J. GRESHAM
MACHEN

J. GRESHAM MACHEN

A Guided Tour
of His Life and Thought

STEPHEN J. NICHOLS

P&R PUBLISHING
P.O. BOX 817 • PHILLIPSBURG • NEW JERSEY 08865-0817

All illustrations appear courtesy of the Machen Archives, Montgomery Library, Westminster Theological Seminary, Philadelphia, Pennsylvania.

Page design and typesetting by Lakeside Design Plus

Printed in the United States of America

Library of Congress Cataloging-in-Publication Data

Nichols, Stephen J., 1970-
    J. Gresham Machen : a guided tour of his life and thought / Stephen J. Nichols.
      p.   cm.
    Includes bibliographical references and index.
    ISBN 0-87552-620-9 (pbk.)
    1. Machen, J. Gresham (John Gresham), 1881–1937. I. Title.

BX9225.M24N53 2004
285'.1'092—dc22
[B]   2004053902

For Ian Keith Nichols
Born May 16, 2004

*May you grow to appreciate and embrace
the rich heritage of Christ's church.*

CONTENTS

ILLUSTRATIONS

ACKNOWLEDGMENTS

I t is my pleasure to thank Grace Mullen at the Montgomery Library, Westminster Theological Seminary, for expertly guiding me through the voluminous archives, offering helpful comments on the outline and manuscript, and sharing her enthusiasm for the subject. Rich Michael, wisely choosing to write his master's thesis on Machen, prompted me to read Machen again, and more than likely led me to write this book. Dale Mort not only reads every word I write, he also offers his never-ending encouragement. The faculty concerns committee at Lancaster Bible College graciously granted some release time, enabling me to write. Jerry Lincoln and the library staff at the college went the extra mile in securing books and materials. The library staff at Westminster proved invaluable, as did Robert Benedetto and the staff of the archives and special collections at Princeton Theological Seminary.

This book would simply not be possible without the support and companionship of my wife, Heidi. To her I am most grateful. Finally, this book is dedicated to our son, Ian Keith Nichols, born May 16, 2004. I promise that I'll not only give you books, I'll also buy you a football. Machen would like that.

INTRODUCTION

J. Gresham Machen's early years surpassed what may be called a typical childhood. His father, Arthur W. Machen, from a politically connected family, rose to prominence as a Baltimore attorney. His mother, Mary Gresham Machen ("Minnie," as her friends called her), possessed an even greater pedigree than her husband, hailing from one of Georgia's elite families. Possessing all the qualities of her genteel upbringing, she felt at home among Baltimore's high society. In 1903 Macmillan published her book, *The Bible in Browning*, which reflects her love of Victorian poetry and the sacred Scriptures. The result of this upbringing was that Machen grew up surrounded by books, connected to social circles—later as a student at Princeton he would be a frequent dinner guest of then current president of the university and future President of the United States Woodrow Wilson, an old family friend—and positioned for a considerable education and a promising career.

Nevertheless, one could scarcely predict that Machen would be at the center of a theological and cultural controversy that would tumble through the first decades of the twentieth century, continuing to leave its mark in the twenty-first. Neither would one likely foresee that he would be the founder of a seminary, a mission agency, and a denomination. Hindsight shows all of this to be the case. But

if we were to catch a glimpse of young Machen, our antici-
pation of his life's course would no doubt miss the mark.
While he made the most of his upbringing and level of privilege, by the time he reached his early adulthood he entirely
lacked a vision for his life. With a B.A. in hand from Johns
Hopkins, he toured Europe, attended classes in banking and
international law at the University of Chicago, and, by his
own account, rejected a future in the clergy—"the ministry,"
he informed his father, "I am afraid I can't think of." Such
driftiness may be chalked up to youth, yet his underlying
ambivalence, especially in regard to things of divinity, would
certainly catch our eye.

We must also take into account Machen's disposition. He
was prone to what polite company refers to as eccentrici-
ties. While years later his behaviors, such as thudding his
head against the wall while lecturing, would endear him to
his students, such demonstrations might give us pause to
place him at the head of such institutions as seminaries and
denominations.

Yet (and herein lies one of the ironies of his life) these apparent detractors, his ambivalence and temperament, became precisely the agents through which Machen was cata-
pulted to the forefront in the fundamentalist and modernist
controversy, and they even became the means by which his
contribution to that controversy stands out in its unique and
astounding way. To put the entire matter briefly, Machen
emerges as a rather unlikely hero. In fact, Machen's is the
classic story of the underdog. His cause was right, his arguments were right, yet he fought such a labyrinthine machine
that, from the beginning, the unfavorable outcome was
predictable.

Though Machen is not as well known as the towering figure from the Protestant Reformation, Machen's path mir-
rors Martin Luther's in uncanny ways. They both found

themselves unwanted by the churches they were ordained in, loved, and lived for. And they both found themselves unwanted for exactly the same reason: calling into question the drift and departure from theological moorings and biblical foundations. They both faced heresy trials—though admittedly Machen's life was never at stake—and both went on to found new denominations. They both also left behind a legacy of biblical and theological scholarship, and both serve as role models for those desirous of defending the faith.

Ironically, their lives ended in a similar fashion as well. Luther, called away to settle a dispute in the fledgling church in the town of his birth, Eisleben, took ill along the trip. He was run-down, on the verge of exhaustion from his tireless efforts at helping the young and fragile church stand firmly. After an apparent recovery, the illness proved too much as it assailed him once again, taking his life. Machen, too, was called away to settle a dispute. He was not summoned to the town of his birth, the bustling city of Baltimore, but to a rural town near Bismarck, North Dakota. But he was there to help a very young church in a very young denomination. By all accounts, he, too, was tired, run-down by his work. He contracted pneumonia, succumbing to it on the day the new year began in 1937.

Luther's body was returned from the town of Eisleben to his adopted city, Wittenberg. As the town's favorite son, he was buried with all fanfare in the town church. Machen's body was returned to the town of his birth, to Baltimore, absent the fanfare. Yet in the press—including all the major metropolitan papers—his death certainly did not go unnoticed. Pearl S. Buck, the famous missionary to China and novelist, and Machen's antagonist as well, lamented in *The New Republic*, "The church has lost a colorful figure and a mind which stimulated by its constant contrary activities.

He added life to the church, and it needs life. And we have all lost something in him." So too follows the estimate of the famed journalist H. L. Mencken, though he never could agree with Machen's theology. In his obituary for Machen, Mencken in typical fashion noted that the odious Calvinism for which Machen so valiantly fought "occupies a place, in my cabinet of private horrors, not far removed from cannibalism." Yet Mencken felt compelled to admire—he said, "greatly admire"—and honor Machen and his life's work. He hailed him as a scholar and theologian, dubbing him *Doctor Fundamentalis* and likening him to the Matterhorn.

What was it about Machen's life that brought forth such praise by his enemies and detractors at his death? Perhaps many factors can be considered. His was a sterling education: undergraduate from Johns Hopkins, with graduate work at the University of Chicago, at Princeton University, at Princeton Theological Seminary, and in Germany. He authored such scholarly achievements as *The Origin of Paul's Religion*, *The Virgin Birth of Christ*, and the classic theological work *Christianity and Liberalism*. After leaving Princeton Seminary after twenty-three years of teaching, he founded Westminster Theological Seminary in 1929. After his bouts with the Presbyterian Church in the U.S.A. over liberalism in the church's missionary work, he founded the Independent Board of Presbyterian Foreign Missions in 1933. And after his dismissal from the denomination, he founded the Orthodox Presbyterian Church in 1936—just months before his death.

But there is much more to Machen the biblical scholar and theologian, Machen the educator and administrator, and Machen the cleric and denominational leader. He corresponded with sitting presidents and governors and national park directors. He testified before Congress against the establishment of the Department of Education, and he protested jaywalking laws before the Philadelphia City Council. During World War I, he left his safe and placid environs at Princeton to serve in the YMCA, running a canteen for French and then American soldiers, lending them his books and preaching, and doing whatever else he could to ease the pains of war for the foot soldiers thrust into combat. Before and after the war, he made numerous trips to Europe, biking hundreds of miles and hiking miles of mountains. His writings also found their way to the editorial pages of *The New York Times*. And his heresy trial became front-page news.

Machen lived a truly remarkable life. In the chapters that follow, these various aspects come to light as the multifaceted nature of his life and work is displayed. This tour of Machen's life and work as scholar, citizen, and churchman is intended as only an introduction. Its intent is to sufficiently whet readers' appetite to send them looking for more.

This year marks the seventy-fifth anniversary of just one of the institutions brought to life through the labors of J. Gresham Machen. On the occasion of the opening of Westminster Theological Seminary, Machen remarked that "it will be hardly attended by those who seek the plaudits of the world or the plaudits of a worldly church." He then offered the reason:

> Our new institution is devoted to an unpopular cause; it is devoted to the service of One who is despised and rejected by the world and increasingly belittled by the visible church, the majestic Lord and Saviour who is presented to us in the Word of God. From him men are turning away one by one. His sayings are too hard, his deeds of power too strange, his atoning death too great an offense to human pride. But to him, despite all, we hold.

A fitting summary that well captures Machen's legacy. Despite all, he held to Christ.

PART 1

MACHEN: A BIOGRAPHY

This section explores the life of J. Gresham Machen, setting the stage and providing a context for the rest of the chapters to follow. Machen began his life in Baltimore, then moved on to Princeton, spending his final years in Philadelphia, though he was hardly bound to these cities. A world traveler, he spent significant time overseas, for graduate study and for service in World War I, as well as for mountain-climbing excursions. Three chapters treat this eventful life. The first traces Machen's intellectual, spiritual, and professional development as he grew up in the genteel Victorian culture of old Baltimore, moved through university and graduate studies, and, after some time of soul-searching, landed as a New Testament professor at Princeton Theological Seminary. Chapter 2 follows Machen through the tumultuous 1920s and the waves of controversy that entangled him, leaving him, at the end of the decade, no longer welcome at Princeton. In the final chapter, we see both triumph and tragedy, as Machen founded three institutions—Westminster Theological Seminary, the Independent Board of Foreign Missions, and the Orthodox Presbyterian Church (originally named the Presbyterian Church of America)—and as he was tried and defrocked as a minister in the Presbyterian Church in the U.S.A.

1

COMING OF AGE

1881–1919

> *We have come upon a very different age from any that preceded us . . . . This is nothing short of a new social age, a new era of human relationship, a new stage-setting for the drama of life.*
>
> *Woodrow Wilson, 1912*

In the winter months of 1936, J. Gresham Machen delivered a series of radio addresses in Philadelphia. Previously, he had delivered addresses on the nature of humanity and sin. Now he was finishing a series on God and on Christ. Though a New Testament scholar by training, and quite an active churchman as of late by circumstance, these lectures find him walking his audience through the basics of Christian doctrine. His very last talk, aired on the final Sunday of the year, closes with these words: "I trust that you have had a very joyous Christmas and I trust that the new year which is so soon to begin may be to you a very blessed year under the mercy of God."

Though Machen had no idea at the time, the only day that he was to see of the new year, 1937, would be the first.

1.1. A young Machen, age five, shows his prowess at geography. "By Gresham Nov. 1886" is written by his mother.

He prerecorded the lectures that were aired and then boarded a train for North Dakota. Machen once wrote that he would never take an airplane, rendering the following opinion: "All I can say is that I wouldn't lower myself by going up in one of the stupid, noisy things." He far preferred the train. Sometimes he took the Baltimore & Ohio; other times it was the Pennsylvania Railroad or the Chesapeake & Ohio—he liked the variety. On this long trip across the country, he first passed through the Allegheny Mountains, a sight that always brought him joy. Then it was on through the Midwest, stopping at Chicago. Perhaps as he passed the city he remembered his summer spent there as a graduate student studying banking and international law. He would have lived a far different life had he pursued that route. Instead, he had taken the direction of biblical scholarship and the ministry, and now he was traveling to smooth over troubled waters in the new denomination, the one that he had by and large founded, and one that was merely a few months old.

As the train pulled out of Chicago, heading to North Dakota, Machen was tired. His colleagues at Westminster Seminary had failed to convince him to spend the winter break getting some much-needed rest. As he arrived in North Dakota, rest was not on the agenda. He assumed a rigorous speaking schedule that, coupled with below-freezing temperatures, resulted in pneumonia. Realizing that death was near, he sent a final telegram to his friend back at Westminster, John Murray: "I am so thankful for [the] active obedience of Christ. No hope without it." Grasping doctrine, and specifically the doctrine of Christ, at the last, Machen died on January 1, 1937.

North Dakota was an unlikely place for Machen to be. He had been raised in Baltimore, and except for his studies abroad and briefly at Chicago, he had spent his days in the

Eastern cities of Baltimore, Princeton, and Philadelphia. Being the de facto head of a church, as he was at the time of his death, was also an unlikely role for him to be playing. Just as he had no idea that the year of 1937 would elude him, so too he had no idea of the life that he was to live as he was a child growing up in the home of Arthur and Minnie Machen on West Monument Street among the stately Victorian townhomes of old Baltimore.

Son of Baltimore

Machen's father first came to Baltimore as a bachelor lawyer determined to build a successful practice. His family had some connections: his father, Lewis Machen, was the chief clerk to the United States Senate, but Arthur Machen struck out on his own, determined to build a law practice. As a law student at Harvard, Arthur turned to writing detective stories to pay the bills, and when he arrived at Baltimore in 1853, he had little more than his skills upon which to start his career. After a rocky beginning, he built quite a successful practice as a master of the spoken word, arguing no fewer than 204 cases—a near record at the time. He also continued his interest in the printed word, editing some compilations of stories and acquiring an impressive collection of rare and antiquarian books. And all of these qualities were not lost on his middle son, John Gresham.

Arthur ended his two decades as a bachelor lawyer in Baltimore when he married Mary Gresham, known as Minnie, in 1873. Her family, rooted in Macon, Georgia, exuded old Southern charm and gentility. They were a family of means with fortunes stemming from railroads and cotton mills. A surviving photograph of the parlor in the Machen home in Baltimore reveals that Minnie and her Victorian tastes clearly had the upper hand in the decorating of the home. Gone are any traces of Arthur's bachelor decor. Like her husband, she too shared a devotion to books, evidenced in her 1903 publication of *The Bible in Browning* by the reputable publishing house The Macmillan Company.

Her love for all things Victorian, including the Victorian poetry of Robert Browning, was superseded only by her devotion to the Bible and her desire to inculcate its teachings into her three sons, Arthur, Jr., John Gresham, and Thomas. Careers in law awaited Machen's older and younger brothers, though his own future, even through and beyond his college years, was not so certain. Judging by his early report cards, one could see Machen's future as a scholar. In the 1895–96 school year, Machen ranked first in his class in geometry, algebra, Latin, Greek, French, natural science, and English, scoring from a low of 98 to a high of 100—respectable marks and subjects for a fourteen-year-old. A few years previous, in 1892, he had also ranked first in his class in all his subjects except one: conduct. On that count he was third, perhaps a reflection of his commitment to one of his favorite pastimes—"stunting," as he liked to call it.

His mother saved these report cards, as she did a few childhood drawings. When he was four he drew a tree with a fence in the background and a pot of flowers. At the more mature age of five he drew (or more than likely traced) a map of the British Isles, reflecting his later revealed prowess at geography—another subject that found him ranked first in his class. A letter also survives from his fifth year. In all-capital letters, he informs his Aunt Emily that he has acquired a new set of soldiers and a new stamp, and then asks, "When are you coming home," neglecting the question mark, but otherwise perfect in penmanship. Through these scattered papers a faint picture emerges of Machen's childhood, a blend of seriousness and high culture and laughter and pranks. And at the center of this upbringing was the

Bible, the *Shorter Catechism,* and *The Pilgrim's Progress,* all poured into the lives of the Machen boys by their mother. At the age of fifteen, upon making a credible profession of faith, Machen became a full member of Franklin Street Presbyterian Church.

When it was time for Machen to go to college, he elected to stay in Baltimore, attending Johns Hopkins University. Owing to his penchant for Baltimore, his choice of Hopkins, as well as his course of study, may also have had something to do with Basil Gildersleeve, a family friend, fellow member of Franklin Street Presbyterian Church, and eminent professor of classics. Machen's love of Horace and Herodotus stemmed from his father, who often read the classics in the original Greek as a means to relax in the evenings. As with his earlier schooling, Machen excelled at Johns Hopkins. One of his professors, Edward H. Griffin, used a paper he had submitted for a course as a model, noting that "in every respect, the essay is an excellent one." In Machen's senior year, he was elected to Phi Beta Kappa. Time at Hopkins also included editing the school paper, *The Hullabaloo,* membership in the chess club, frequent baseball watching, and, of course, "stunting."

As a graduation present from his parents, Machen took an extended trip to Europe. He visited the museums and toured the streets of Paris and observed the windmills and walked the canals of Bruges. At Antwerp, he saw the paintings of Rubens and Van Dyck, especially moved by the former's "Descent from the Cross," "Raising from the Cross," and "Assumption," displayed not in the museum but in the cathedral. But what struck him most of all were the mountains. He wrote to his mother of the beauty and of "the spectacle of the star-light followed by the sun lighting up the peaks in the morning." His letters home during later trips to Europe also contain frequent references to the impres-

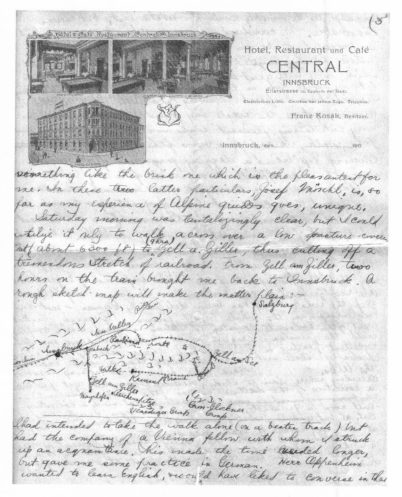

1.2. In a letter to his father, September, 1905, Machen recounts his mountain-climbing exploits, complete with map, before settling down to study under Wilhelm Herrmann in Germany.

sions that the mountains left on him and references to his favorite recreational activity of mountain-climbing.

Much later in his life he wrote an essay on the subject, "Mountains and Why We Love Them," first published in *Christianity Today* in 1934. After recalling his expeditions through the Alps—always, he admits, with the help of a guide—he declares, "I do love the mountains and I have loved them ever since I can remember anything at all." Mountains, he continues in the essay, give us perspective, a vantage point from which we can evaluate both the present and the past, the machinations of humanity and governments, and the impact that we are making in the world. But what they provide most of all is memories. "What have I from my visits to the mountains?" he asks, and then answers his own question by pointing to the memories of comfort: "In hours of darkness and discouragement I love to think of the sharp summit ridge of the Matterhorn piercing the blue [sky] or the majesty and the beauty of the world spread out at my feet when I stood at the summit of the Dent Blanche."

In 1901, the hours and seasons of darkness were yet to fall upon Machen. He was, however, perhaps a little discouraged because he had yet to discover a clear path for his life. Most likely still under the influence of Gildersleeve, Machen decided to remain at Johns Hopkins for a year of graduate study in the classics. He then went to the University of Chicago in the summer of 1902 to study international law and banking, evidence of a listless spirit. After a visit with his pastor back in Baltimore, and frequent conversations with his parents, Machen decided to enroll at Princeton Theological Seminary for a course in divinity, while simultaneously pursuing a graduate philosophy program at Princeton University. He was not, however, embarking on a career in the pastorate. In fact, he enrolled at Princeton only after he had made it quite clear that he was not seeking ordination. "The ministry I am afraid I can't think of," he wrote his father.

Football—and Other Things—at Princeton

From 1902 until 1929, excepting some extended trips abroad due to both studies and World War I, Princeton remained Machen's home. His work as a student did not consume his days. He once wrote, "If we could only lower our average temperature about 15°, how much more I could accomplish." But favorable weather, Princeton football—in his first semester he wrote, "The football at Princeton is a continual delight to me," even though he couldn't get "too painfully excited" about Princeton's often low scores—and Philadelphia baseball all conspired to keep Machen from becoming a bookworm. Sometimes they even managed to tempt him to skip his afternoon Hebrew classes, the beginnings of his philosophical objections to any classes held past the morning hours. He didn't always skip classes for ex-

1.3. The Benham Club, with mascot "Toby," of Princeton Theological Seminary, during Machen's student days. Machen is in the top row, fourth from left.

tracurricular amusement, however. In his first term, he was also invited to the home of Woodrow Wilson, then president of Princeton University, an invitation he had to decline because he was scheduled to deliver a sermon in homiletics class the same day.

Machen lived in Alexander Hall, both as a student and later as a professor. Immediately next door to this large building was the stately home of Benjamin Breckenridge Warfield, dubbed "the Lion of Old Princeton." It was then the practice of Princeton Seminary to provide housing, in addition to a salary, for the faculty. Warfield rarely left his home, except to teach his courses and attend church. His wife suffered severe health problems, living out her years at Princeton mostly as an invalid. Warfield tended to her, and he wrote prodigiously, leaving his own literary legacy later published in a ten-volume collection. The rest of the faculty was no less impressive. George Tybout Purves held sway in the New Testament department, Geerhardus Vos had just completed the first of four decades of teaching biblical theology, and Caspar Wistar Hodge Jr. carried on the long family tradition in systematic theology.

Two members of the faculty made particular impact on Machen: Francis Landey Patton and William Park Armstrong. Patton was simultaneously president of the university and professor at the seminary. Raised in Bermuda, Patton exuded Old World gentlemanly manners, no less matched by his deftness in the classroom and pulpit. A student notebook from Patton's course in theism has the following inscription on the inside cover: "In response to a petition from the students, Dr. Patton delivered these lectures in Miller Chapel, Mar 25–29, 1907. The chapel was crowded full from the beginning to the end of the course." The student then added, "A most impressive time at Princeton!"

Despite his ability in the classroom, Patton had his share of difficulties. In 1902 he was effectively removed from the presidency of the university, being replaced by Woodrow Wilson. Patton retained his professorship in the university and became the first president of Princeton Theological Seminary. Before 1902, since its founding in 1812, the seminary had been run by faculty committee with the senior professor leading, a role falling mostly to Charles Hodge and Warfield. Curiously, Machen adopted this same practice when he founded Westminster Theological Seminary in 1929. When Patton assumed the office at the seminary, he largely kept the prior format, not letting his title change or the new position disrupt the status quo of a faculty-run institution. This changed with Patton's successor, J. Ross Stevenson, who served as president of the seminary from 1914 to 1936. Stevenson took a much more active role as president. Machen, as well as many others on the faculty, at first viewed Stevenson suspiciously, then came to respect him, and later came to see him as bringing about the end of Old Princeton. Machen sorely missed Patton. At the time of Patton's death in 1932, Machen wrote, "He was to me the truest friend. I could have never gone forward at all without his help."

Machen also benefited from the help of William Park Armstrong. "Army," as his friends knew him, taught Machen New Testament, and he immediately recognized the potential in his pupil. After later joining the faculty at Princeton and becoming Army's colleague, Machen spent many Sunday afternoons having dinner with his family. Writing years later, William Armstrong's son, who had been just a young boy at the time, recalled, "[Machen] really was a most delightful person full of good humor and laughter and ready with a story. I can still hear the ring of his and my father's laugh at the dinner table or in my father's study as they talked or shared their views." Armstrong was from the South, Selma, Alabama, and had just begun his tenure at Princeton when Machen arrived. Like his student, Armstrong was a member of the Southern Presbyterian Church, but found himself teaching in the North. It was Armstrong, along with Francis Patton, who advocated for Machen to win the Maitland Prize for his work on the birth narratives in the gospels. This highly competitive prize had two elements: publication of one's work in the *Princeton Theological Review*—Machen's work was published as a two-part article entitled "The New Testament Account of the Birth of Jesus," his first publication—and a fellowship for a year's study in Germany.

Year of Crisis

Machen, with his customary ambivalence during this time of his life, went to Germany, though he relied on his own funds, contrary to the protestations of Armstrong. During the academic year 1905–06, Machen enrolled first at Marburg and then at Göttingen. Before he settled into the rigors of study, he took an extensive bicycle tour, stopping along the way for a fair share of mountain-climbing. Much has been made of this time at Germany as a time of severe crisis for Machen. The ambiguities of his future continued to dominate his letters home, only now they contained the added dimension of spiritual unrest. Darryl Hart, however, has pointed out that this was not the first time Machen had struggled with issues of his faith. In fact, Machen himself wrote, "It was not Germany . . . that first brought doubts into my soul." Nevertheless, Germany, and largely the lectures by Wilhelm Herrmann at Marburg, proved a challenge for Machen. Well trained by his Princeton professors to engage liberalism in the arena of biblical criticism, Machen was not ready for Herrmann's vital piety. "I can't criticize him," Machen exclaimed in a letter to his father, adding, "I have been thrown all into confusion by what he says—so much deeper is his devotion to Christ than anything I have known in myself during the past few years." Yet Herrmann's piety was not rooted in orthodox Christianity.

Interestingly, Herrmann had a similar impact on his two other famous students, Rudolf Bultmann and Karl Barth, although in their cases (especially Bultmann's), they did not see a robust defense of orthodox Christianity as the antidote.

What Machen was searching for was neither an intellectualism devoid of faith nor a faith devoid of intellectual merit. Nor was he after either a rigorous scholarship without piety or a vital piety without roots in scholarship. He longed for piety and intellect fused into one, an intellectually informed and compelling faith. And this is what the year of crisis in Germany led him to grasp. Although his season of doubt was challenging—he once wrote that this soul-searching "always gives me the blues"—he emerged stronger for it and fitted for the challenges to come. Actually, his mother helped him to see this as well. In the course of corresponding during this time, his mother mentioned that she was not in favor of Machen's thinking of staying in Germany to pursue a Ph.D. Machen mistook this remark as her attempt to shield him from further exposure to the liberals or from the further investigation of faith. He winced at the prospect. On September 14, 1906, having just returned from Germany, he told his father that he was "distressed," thinking that his mother did not have "faith enough in the truth of her religion to be willing to open the way to free investigation." It also brought forth a twenty-five-page letter to his mother. She began her reply, dated September 17, 1906: "I understand you far better than ever before. But I am almost hopeless of making you understand me." She continues the mild rebuke:

> My son, my whole life has been a protest against the very position which you suppose me to take. When I was sixteen, I rebelled against the trampling of the intellect. I could not have a blind faith. This required some boldness and independence, for I was little more than a child, and I lived in an environment that discouraged freedom of thought. All my life long I have held that free investigation is the only way to climb to the mountain-top of intelligent faith . . . . I do not and never have looked at free probing for truth as anything to be afraid of. I am [an] apostle of the opposite position. Certainly if a man is to be a scholar and a teacher he cannot investigate too much.

Machen needed to hear these words. He had forgotten the vital piety he had seen in his home and, for that matter, at Princeton. But he also needed to hear that the vital piety was founded on intellectual merit. The faith that Machen would be defending in the years to come would be no blind faith.

39 Alexander Hall

Machen had two teaching offers even before he returned to America. Ethelbert Warfield, president of Lafayette College and brother of Benjamin Breckinridge, offered him a post teaching Greek and German, and Armstrong offered him a one-year appointment in New Testament, having convinced the directors of the seminary that he could use some assistance. Machen was considering turning down both offers and pursuing other studies, possibly in a field other than theological or biblical studies. In the end, he accepted the appointment to Princeton, though ambivalently. Following

1.4. A receipt for books, his and his family's avocation, while a student in Germany, June 8, 1906.

his father's advice, he likely thought of it as a means to bide time. His father had encouraged him, "For the present, acceptance of the offered field at Princeton for a year would be advisable, giving time for consideration and a final decision later which was initially only a year appointment," adding, "Don't imagine that your past studies would be lost in any event. You have had valuable intellectual training which will serve a good purpose whatever field of life's work may be assigned to you. . . . You are abundantly young enough for any fresh start."

By 1907, something about life and work at Princeton appealed to Machen, and he decided to stay. Having taken the train for a quick trip to New York City, he stopped by Brooks Brothers, purchased a new suit and a tuxedo for $133, and began his career. He took on new courses, including seminars on the birth narratives of Christ in the gospels, a subject that was quickly becoming his lifelong pursuit and would eventually result in the publication of *The*

Virgin Birth of Christ in 1930. He also became quite popular among the students, not only because of his brilliance as a lecturer and his mastery of the field, but also because of his rather eccentric antics, then only beginning. The stuff of student stories for years to come, these included thumping his head against the wall while he lectured and reading the newspaper while his students parsed Greek verbs out loud— still being able to hear mistakes, correct them, and keep on reading.

They also appreciated him for what he did outside the classroom. He lived in the student dorm, 39 Alexander Hall, on the third floor. On Saturday evenings, he would throw open his door and the students would pile in, accepting his rather intriguing combination of fresh fruit and tobacco— he once said, "My idea of delight is a Princeton room full of fellows smoking." His correspondence files are full of letters from past students—usually bearing interesting nicknames, such as "Fat" and "Birdie," along with Machen's own "Das"—reminiscing about the "pleasant things of Princeton." These letters update on marriages, employment, travel, all the usual items. The letters also ask for lyrics to songs of which the writer can remember only a few lines, such as "Der Kaiser ist ein guter Mann," and "I'm a soldier boy, Lizette," or one that ends, "Of money he will have plenty, a fortune he will spend, he will buy a home and settle down, in dear old Ireland." Not all was business in 39 Alexander Hall.

But all was not well at Princeton, either. Not too long into Machen's tenure, a student rebellion broke out at the seminary in 1909. (A similar rebellion had occurred earlier in the 1800s, which, as historian Mark Noll has shown, probably had something to do with the weeks of severe winter weather and freezing temperatures.) The revolt had much to do with the curriculum and the teaching. The students wanted more electives in Old Testament, they wanted more practical courses in the curriculum, and they chafed under the teaching of Armstrong, who used too much Latin and Greek, and Patton, whose lectures were too impractical. The students were so entrenched that a large section of the junior class threatened not to return, and they sent lengthy missives to the board of directors. Patton, as president, led the charge for the faculty's response. Patton offered a point-by-point rebuttal, at times sounding exasperated, as when he exclaimed rhetorically, "Haven't we a learned ministry any more?" Machen was nowhere implicated by the students. In fact, he himself favored a more elective curriculum—perhaps remembering his listless spirit as a seminarian—against the likes of Warfield and Patton. But with the call for a more practical preparation Machen could not concur. The rebellion soon came to an end. The demands of the students, however, would reemerge in the ensuing decades, and when they did, they would be met by a much more acquiescent administration.

Now along in his career as a scholar, Machen added the credential of clergy, receiving ordination in 1914, also being promoted from instructor to assistant professor. His inaugural address, "History and Faith," was widely distributed, and it has also been widely reprinted, occurring most recently in the anthology *American Sermons* by The Library of America. The responses poured in from around the world. Henry van Dyke, who was on leave from Princeton University where he taught literature to serve as the ambassador to the Netherlands and Luxembourg during the Wilson administration, offered his congratulations, as did former students and colleagues at other institutions. Machen's reputation also came to the attention of Union Seminary in Virginia. He declined its offer of a position, since by now he was a confirmed Princetonian. "At present

I am so deeply rooted in Princeton," he wrote, "by a good many ties, that it is impossible for me to accept even the great opportunity which would be mine if I should be called to the chair in Richmond."

The threat of liberalism caused tremors on the larger front as well. The challenge grew so strong that brothers Lyman and Milton Stewart, who had made their fortunes in oil, enlisted such luminaries as R. A. Torrey and A. C. Dixon to edit an originally twelve-volume paperback series to defend Christianity entitled *The Fundamentals*, published 1910–15 and distributed by the millions free to Christian workers and ministers. This work brought together such a hybrid of scholars so as to include both B. B. Warfield and C. I. Scofield among the contributors. By many accounts, it offered the first crystallized expression of fundamentalism. These Herculean efforts reflected the urgent need to respond to liberalism's impact on the church.

A Very Different Age

When Woodrow Wilson was campaigning for President, having left Princeton for a stop at the governor's mansion of New Jersey along the way, he began one speech by observing, "We have come upon a very different age from any that preceded us." He had in mind the changing face of the economy from ongoing industrialization and the rise of corporations. But when he said these words, as well the words, "Now this is nothing short of a new social age, a new era of human relationships, a new stage-setting for the drama of life," he could have just as easily been talking about the church and theology. What was also true, although Wilson did not realize it at the time, was that "the very different age" that he was seeing in America was also occurring across the face of Europe, and within five years, America would join in the fray of World War I.

Machen, well beyond the age for the recently instituted draft, nevertheless wanted to contribute to the war effort. He considered the chaplaincy, but decided against it, thinking that his rank as officer would keep him from ministering to the foot soldiers. He also, like so many other intellectuals such as Ernest Hemingway, looked into being an ambulance driver. By the time he was considering that, however, there was such an abundance of volunteers that, while being promised an assignment to humanitarian efforts, they were instead being deployed to transport munitions. Machen still wanted to serve, however, so he went with the YMCA. That organization played an active role in the war in many ways. It offered education and literacy programs for soldiers, provided guidance on moral issues and spiritual counseling, and ran "huts" or canteens, offering sandwiches, cigarettes, coffee, and reading materials for soldiers coming off the front. Machen supplemented the magazines with his own books, keeping a careful ledger of the books loaned to French soldiers. The names of Arnout, Lepage, Tribault, Lt. Dumont, and Sgt. Bernard are joined by many others who enjoyed Machen's books, an oasis in the midst of the horrors of war. He also frequently led Bible studies among the soldiers, not having much success in conducting Sunday services.

Machen served faithfully, for most of the time in the "Army Zone," surrounded by bombs, the never-ending exchange of gunfire, and the din of airplanes overhead. Machen went along with the unit of French and then American soldiers, moving with them as they either were bombed out of their encampment or simply moved about as the front line meandered back and forth through the intractable vicissitudes of war. He walked past devastated villages and the seemingly countless dead on the battlefields and along the bombed-out roads. When the war came to an end on November 11, 1918, Machen remained in France for a few months before returning to the ivy-covered buildings of Princeton. Many historians have noted how the war changed America, evidenced in the title of one history of the war, *The Last Days of Innocence*. It was America's coming of age, and it struck quite a blow to the spirit of the progressive era. The impact of the war was no less in the case of Machen. Stunned by the loss of life and the devastation of landscape, Machen was not the same quiet scholar enjoying his detached academic life.

With World War I over, the battle for the faith was only beginning. Through the first two decades of the twentieth century, Machen had been engaged only in the periphery, and most of the time he was not sure that he wanted to be engaged even at that level. In the next decade, all of that would change. As the "Roaring Twenties" came into full force, Machen emerged as the premier defender of the faith.

2

THE ROARING TWENTIES
1920–1929

*I well know that you are in for a fight and that you will
make enemies.*

Mary Gresham Machen to Her Son

Not much correspondence passed between J. Gresham
Machen and Princeton's elder statesman, Benjamin
B. Warfield. This should not be surprising, since
they worked together and were just as likely to have long
conversations as to write long letters. But the few letters that
exist, mostly notes from Warfield to Machen, are telling. In
a congratulatory letter on Machen's publications, Warfield
relays, "I read them greedily at once." In another, perhaps
prophetic, letter, Warfield exhorts his junior colleague, "The
work you are doing is so valuable to the church. . . . I beg
you to hold firmly on your course. We must not lose this
course." Even more telling of the relationship between the
two are the letters Machen sent to his mother on the occasion of Warfield's death. "Princeton will seem an insipid
place without him," he mourns, adding, "There is no one
living in the church capable of occupying one quarter of his

place. To me, he was an incalculable help and support in a hundred different ways."

A few days later in another letter to his mother, Machen recalls his final conversation with Warfield. Machen remi-

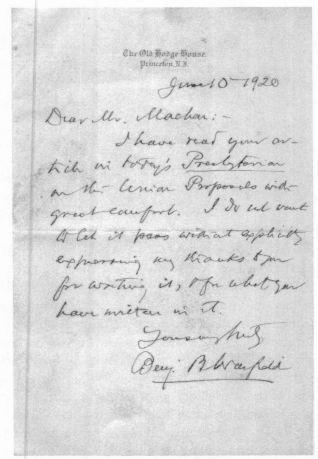

2.1. A brief, but typical, letter from B. B. Warfield to Machen, June 10, 1920.

Dear Mr. Machen. I have read your article in today's *Presbyterian* on the Union proposals with great comfort. I do not want to let it pass without explicitly expressing my thanks to you for writing it. & for what you have written in it. Yours very truly. Benj. B. Warfield

nisces how he expressed his hope that there might be a "split in the church in order to separate the Christians from the anti-Christian propagandists," to which Warfield replied, "No, you can't split rotten wood." As Machen interpreted it, "His expectation seemed to be that the organized church, dominated by naturalism, would become so cold and dead, that people would come to see that spiritual life could be found only outside of it, and that thus there might be a new beginning." What Warfield also more than likely realized, perhaps pointing his remark in that final conversation toward this end, was that his younger colleague would be at the center of the new beginning. In the same letter to his mother, Machen, recalling the carrying out of Warfield's casket from First Presbyterian Church, lamented, "It seems to me that the old Princeton—a great institution it was—died when Dr. Warfield was carried out." The death of Warfield and of Old Princeton, however, meant a new beginning, with a new leader. Though he would be the first to see himself as well below Warfield's stature, the mantle fell on Machen.

Machen had published a number of articles and an extensive series of Sunday school lessons for the Presbyterian Church in the U.S.A., but it was 1921 when his first book, *The Origin of Paul's Religion,* came out, published by Macmillan. The book stemmed from his courses at Princeton and from a series of lectures he had delivered at Union Theological Seminary in Virginia. It is of no little significance that Machen's first book treated issues of New Testament scholarship. Though he is known today much more widely for his book *Christianity and Liberalism,* which was *1923* to appear two years later, this first book represents well the type of contribution that Machen made to the fundamentalist and modernist controversy. Robust, rigorous, and responsible scholarship would mark all his efforts in defending the faith. A better successor to Warfield could not be found.

In addition to his writing, he had his full share of speaking, especially from 1920 on. One such invitation concerned an Easter address for the Business Women's luncheon, sponsored by the Women's Conservation Committee on Madison Avenue in New York City. In businesslike fashion, Isabelle Davis, who would preside over the meetings, sent Machen a detailed rundown of the day's events:

> The plan of the luncheon is this. The girls are quickly served in a room on the ground floor, and pass immediately upstairs for the meeting. While there is some coming and going during the time you are speaking, it is not very marked and the girls give the most rapt attention.
>
> We have about ten minutes of singing and a few notices, then the speaker from fifteen to twenty minutes and then the singing again, the notices, then the speaker for another period of from fifteen to twenty minutes, and so on until the speaker has given four addresses. If you would come promptly at ten minutes of twelve, it would be possible for you to leave at a quarter of two.

He was further asked to repeat his first address in the third time slot and his second in the fourth to accommodate the business girls' getting back to the office. He delivered another speaking address that year at the Baccalaureate of Hamden-Sidney College, where he was awarded an honorary Doctor of Divinity degree in 1921.

After the ceremony, Dr. Machen drove his Hudson up the Atlantic coast to Seal Harbor, Maine, where his family spent their summers. Since Machen's childhood days, his family had spent their extended vacation on the Maine coast. It was also there that he met the one romance of his life, though a relationship was not in the offing. While they corresponded throughout their lives and maintained a friendship, she was a Unitarian, and so Machen remained a bachelor. Around September, the summer breezes off the Atlantic Ocean cooled and Machen, taking his car to the Seaside Inn Garage for one final maintenance check, drove south for the start of a new semester. In 1922 his salary at Princeton increased from $2,888.88 to $3,004.62. He spent ten dollars of it to pay his admission fee to the Appalachian Mountain Club in October.

The Watershed Year

No rest came to Machen during the 1922–23 academic year. It seems that he was making good on his wartime commitment to apply himself assiduously to his task. Two new books appeared, as well as a reissue of yet another. He had his courses and faculty responsibilities to contend with at the seminary, and he kept a speaking schedule that would rival those on the conference circuit. His annual report on his activities, submitted to Charles Erdman at Princeton, tediously recalls his speaking. It tires one simply to read it. On October 8, he gave an address commemorating the first meeting of the American Revision Committee at Union College in Schenectady, New York. He spoke to Methodists in New Jersey, an interdenominational minister's group in Philadelphia, and groups in New York City and as far away as Iowa.

The first month of the new year afforded Machen eight different speaking engagements, and then in February it was off to Chicago to speak during Founder's Week at Moody. Bible institutes, colleges, churches, and presbyteries all heard Machen through the spring months. Not all his engagements were headliners. He spent sixteen Monday evenings teaching in the community school of religious education at the YMCA in Trenton, New Jersey. No longer an obscure New Testament professor quietly laboring in his study, Machen was brought in the decade of the 1920s to the center of attention, not only in the Presbyterian circles that one might expect of a Princeton professor, but in the larger arenas of both the academic and the fundamentalist worlds. His name was appearing more and more in *The New York Times.* Though more intriguing events were on the horizon for the later years, there can be no doubt: 1923 was a watershed year in Machen's life.

First, the book that was to get wide use and appreciation, even by those who disagreed with Machen, came from the presses at Macmillan, *New Testament Greek for Beginners.* This book, probably enjoyed much more by instructors than by students, has accompanied and continues to accompany college and seminary students as they trek through the maze of Koine or common Greek, the language of the New Testament. When the book first came out, it was quite welcomed by Greek instructors. Roland Bainton at Yale wrote to Machen to express his indebtedness for the book and to discuss Bainton's own desire to someday publish a manual of Greek reading exercises. Bainton never published that book; he moved on to church history, writing a magisterial biography of Martin Luther instead. The need for Machen's grammar grew out of his own teaching of the subject when he first started his career at Princeton. His love for languages had come long before Princeton, owing to his parents' inculcating in him a fondness for reading Latin, Greek, and French. Years later, when he founded Westminster Theological Seminary, he spoke of the institution's purpose of "training specialists in the Bible." To Machen's mind, a minister must know Greek (and, he would add, Hebrew). The currents swirling about him, insisting on more practical issues of ministerial preparation, only served to further en-

2.2. J. Gresham Machen with Harold McAfee Robinson, c. 1921

trench his view. While it is his other book published in 1923, *Christianity and Liberalism,* that jumps to mind as we consider Machen's legacy, given his commitment to a well-trained clergy and his stress on the biblical languages, *New Testament Greek for Beginners* certainly has its place as well. And incidentally, like *Christianity and Liberalism,* this book is also dedicated to his mother.

Machen received numerous congratulatory letters for all his books. Mostly the letter-writers insisted that he not reply because they simply wanted to express their appreciation and not tax him for a response. But he typically ignored their admonitions and sent a brief note. A fascinating example is a letter from Leonora Harnbreche of Illinois, who was studying Greek for herself when she had the good fortune to find Machen's grammar. While interested in the common Greek language of the New Testament, she also desired to read the Attic Greek of the classic authors "with profit and pleasure," expressing that "ever since a child I have had the desire to know something of the Greek language, which I heard spoken of as the language of poets." She could not have sent such a letter to a more eager recipient. Forgoing his typical brief reply, Machen sent off a lengthy letter exclaiming his delight and noting how "refreshing [it is] to find someone who appreciates the study of Greek." He launches into a suggested course of study for learning and reading Greek and ends by saying, "I am particularly pleased at your characterizing my Greek book as

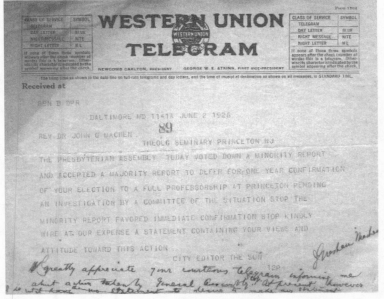

2.3. A telegram from *The Baltimore Sun* requesting Machen's response concerning the action of the General Assembly on Machen's appointment to the chair of apologetics at Princeton. His handwritten reply: "I greatly appreciate your courteous telegram informing me about action taken by [the] General Assembly. Stop. At present, however, I do not desire to make any statement.

J. Gresham Machen"

'friendly'. I hope my students are willing to apply the same adjective to it!" The letter was a bit of an oasis for Machen. His training and his proclivities all pointed to scholarship and the languages—he would be quite content to spend his days corresponding on reading Greek. But he was pulled elsewhere.

The addresses he gave in 1922 and 1923 reveal much about the direction in which he was pulled. Like most engaged in regular public speaking, Machen reused material. Recurring titles and topics include "What Is Christianity?," "The Fundamentals of the Christian Faith," and "Is Christianity True?" These themes reach their ultimate expression in Machen's thought in his classic work, also from 1923, *Christianity and Liberalism.* With this book, Machen emerged as the singular spokesperson for the rigorous defense of orthodox Christianity in response to the challenge of liberalism. In some ways this career path mirrored that of his mentor, Warfield, who had begun his career as a New Testament scholar and then moved to the field of systematic theology.

Even in 1921, Machen's name came up among the board of directors of the seminary for the chair of dogmatic theology. Machen, sending a letter to one of the board members, squashed that recommendation before it even became a topic of business among them. In 1926, the directors would attempt to move him into the chair of apologetics, another move that never came to fruition, only this time due to the machination of the General Assembly of the Presbyterian Church in the U.S.A. It would not be until 1930 that Machen could return to his New Testament scholarship. With Warfield's passing, and others in the fundamentalist camp consumed with issues of eschatology or revivalism or cultural issues such as Prohibition, it fell to Machen to offer the scholarly defense of Christianity.

Warfield, in a discussion of certain developments in church history, once spoke of "the vital processes of controversy," as opposed to "the cool closets of theological construction." Machen's life—that is, his personal, ecclesiastical, and professional life—was not to be one of cool closets. In fact, like his mentor's, Machen's own life, especially since 1923 on, was dominated by controversy. As Warfield's quote points out, however, such controversy possesses a life-giving quality. It is hard to imagine that Machen enjoyed the conflict—though at times his enemies accused him of such *schadenfreude*. It is much more probable that he dreaded it; in fact, his letters reveal that to be the case. Nevertheless, his life and work reflect a certain vitality, a quality that otherwise would probably have never been displayed.

Some of the vitality shines through in Machen's response to a sermon preached by Harry Emerson Fosdick. Fosdick, though an ordained Baptist, was serving at First Presbyterian Church in New York City when he preached his infamous sermon "Shall the Fundamentalists Win?," a battle cry for liberalism. The sermon provided the immediate impetus for Machen's classic, *Christianity and Liberalism*. Despite Machen's clear criticism of Fosdick and liberalism, the new view abounded, picking up momentum. Two significant events spurred it on in 1924: the Auburn Affirmation and the publication of Shailer Mathews's *The Faith of Modernism*. Mathews, who was professor at the University of Chicago Divinity School and past president of the Federal Council of Churches (1912–16), redefined the basics of the Christian faith, making its teachings more palatable for moderns. In his view, the Christian faith must adapt or it will find itself quite out of step. This view calls for the rethinking of the biblical text and revision of key doctrines. Christ, for instance, retains his role in providing salvation, but the exactitude of older Christianity, Mathews argued, should be stripped away. In short, the formulations of Christ as the God-man no longer must be enforced, and the doctrine of the substitutionary atonement of his work on the cross should give way to simply seeing the example of Christ's virtuous sacrifice. Mathews reveals his approach to the Bible when he writes, "If it should appear that certain stories of the Bible were legend rather than sober history, this would simply mean that the past expressed its religious attitude and conviction by the use of legend."

Mathews was a Baptist; he had plenty of counterparts in Presbyterianism. A group of ministers from the Presbyterian Church in the U.S.A. gathered in Auburn, New York, in 1923, and then published their report, "The Auburn Affirmation," in 1924. They were reacting to the "Five Point Deliverance," a statement issued in 1910 that had been reaffirmed at the 1923 General Assembly of the Presbyterian Church—prompting the Auburn meeting. The five points specifically grew out of the liberal challenge to the cardinal doctrines of the faith, including the inerrancy of Scripture, the virgin birth of Christ, the substitutionary atonement, Christ's bodily resurrection, and Christ's miracles during his earthly life. The conservatives within the denomination made these beliefs essential to all candidates seeking ordination. Their concern was that a number of ministers were interpreting the Westminster Standards, the confessional documents of the Presbyterian Church, too loosely.

By May 1924, the engineers of the Auburn Affirmation had garnered over 1,200 signatures opposed to making the Five Point Deliverance necessary for ordination. These tactics of revision and reinterpretation of the Bible and orthodox theology were subtle, going largely unnoticed and unchallenged by a large swath of the church. But Machen was well into the fray. He responded to the work of Mathews and others with his "sequel" to *Christianity and Liberalism*, *What Is Faith?*, published by Macmillan in 1925. And Machen was not alone.

Students Standing for Faith

In the days leading up to Thanksgiving 1925, seminary students, professors, and churchmen held the first conference of the League of Evangelical Students for five days on the campus of Calvin College and at Wealthy Street Baptist Church in Grand Rapids, Michigan. More than 200 students from American seminaries revealed their commitment to orthodox theology by joining with the League during its first year. And at its first meeting, Machen numbered among the speakers, lending his enthusiastic support. Modeled after the Student Volunteer Movement of a few decades earlier, this group of committed ministerial students actually began through the efforts of Princeton Seminary students, with no little controversy surrounding it.

At the time of its formation, Charles Erdman, professor of practical theology at Princeton, served as adviser to the student organization. The organization had ties to other seminaries that were quickly moving in a liberal direction, which prompted the Princetonians to conceive of a new league. Erdman at first appeared supportive, but then withdrew his backing. The students then looked to the faculty to appoint a new faculty adviser, and they chose Machen. In the process, however, Erdman accused Machen of engineering the thing, which was the report that made headlines in *The New York Times* and other papers. Eventually, Machen would be vindicated, and eventually, though having shaky beginnings, the League would go on to be a source of joy for Machen. He once spoke of the League as the salient example of "the type of Christianity that responds with full abandon of the heart and life to the Savior's redeeming love, that is willing to bear all things for Christ's sake, that has a passion for the salvation of souls, that holds the Bible to be, not partly true and partly false, but all true, the blessed, holy Word of God." One of the young students who played a key role in the formation of the League was Ned Stonehouse, Machen's protégé and later biographer.

This Bitter Hour

But these times of joy for Machen were encountered in what Stonehouse refers to as Machen's "Valley of Humiliation." Strife and controversy marked the entire last decade of Machen's life, and it was played out in the national arena. Even the controversy at First Presbyterian Church in Princeton, New Jersey, in 1923 and 1924 received national attention. Machen was serving as stated supply for the church when Henry van Dyke—literature professor at Princeton University, former Presbyterian minister, former

2.4. Though barely seen in the back row, Machen played a prominent role in the League of Evangelical Students, a group of which is pictured here.

United States ambassador, and renowned author—gave up his pew. And he sent a copy of the letter that he sent to First Presbyterian's elders to *The New York Times*. He blasted Machen, reporting that the few Sundays he is free from speaking "are too precious to be wasted in listening to such a dismal, bilious travesty of the gospel." Van Dyke added, "What [Machen] says is untrue and malicious. Until he is done, count me out, and give up my pew in the church." The story made the rounds in the newspapers, garnering front-page headlines in some cities. When Machen of his own choosing stepped down from the pulpit, he was replaced by Charles Erdman. Van Dyke returned to his pew, and again he made it a press event. This "van Dyke incident," as it has come to be called, is simply a portrait in miniature of the larger battles that Machen contended with at Princeton Seminary and in his denomination.

In his insightful and scholarly study of the modernist controversy in the Presbyterian Church, historian Bradley Longfield argues that the real problem within the church was ultimately due not to the modernists or liberals, but to the moderates, whom Machen referred to as "indifferentists." He explains how the moderates, driven by an almost desperate sense of maintaining unity, cultivated an environment of tolerance—tolerance except, of course, of the hard-liner fundamentalists. And no one fits the bill better in this regard than Machen's colleague at Princeton, Charles Rosenbury Erdman. The clash between Machen and Erdman had its beginnings in the van Dyke incident, gained momentum through the League of Evangelical Students, and came to a head in the Princeton Seminary controversy in the latter half of the 1920s.

Erdman, having been narrowly defeated in his bid for moderator of the General Assembly in 1924, was elected moderator in 1925. He filled important committees and boards with conservatives, liberals, and moderates, reflecting his tendency to placate the factions. When a potentially schismatic action involving the ordination of two ministers who denied the virgin birth came before the assembly, Erdman had the matter turned over to a committee for further investigation rather than defrock them, an action that endeared him to the liberal cause and to Henry Sloane Coffin, then pastor of Madison Avenue Presbyterian Church and soon president of Union Theological Seminary in New York. On his appointment to the moderatorship, telegrams and letters poured in congratulating Erdman. One even came from his friend, the famous evangelist Billy Sunday: "I do not believe you are a modernist. I do not believe you are among those who deny the Virgin birth of Jesus, as some say," adding, "I have no respect for these intellectual engineers who try to chart man's pathway through this sin-cursed world by the compass of their own opinions, nor for these theological chemists who would dissolve the atoning blood of Jesus into mist and vapor." The letter continues, lambasting modernism and extolling the virtues of the "old-fashioned religion."

Sunday, however, apparently entertained suspicions regarding Erdman's fitness for the post, as revealed in a letter he sent to Machen the same month. "Some time at your convenience," Sunday inquired, "I wish you would write me and tell me confidentially what this discussion is about concerning the candidacy of Dr Erdman for the moderatorship. What is the basis for the talk about his alleged Modernism, I'd like to know just what the crux of the matter is." Machen obliged, noting that those who oppose Erdman do not do so "because they have any criticism of his orthodoxy." Instead, it is due to "his compromising" attitude by allowing the liberal presence to remain in the church. Machen continued, "If his policy of palliation and concealment of the issue is continued only a very few years, our church will be in control of the enemies of the gospel." Sunday replied, somewhat ambivalently, "I do not know a man whom personally I am more delighted to have honored with the moderatorship. Yet I do not think I ever can see how much can be accomplished by conciliation as far as Modernism is concerned. I think the fact that we have been tolerant is the reason this weed has already grown so noxious." Sunday was right in his assessment of the current state, and Machen proved accurate in his prediction for the near future.

The General Assembly in 1926 proved no more favorable to the conservative cause in general and to Machen in particular. The board of directors at Princeton Seminary approved the promotion of Machen to the chair of apologetics. As a perfunctory matter, the promotion was brought before the General Assembly for approval. The assembly, however, delayed action on the matter, a not-so-veiled insult. Machen got a number of conciliatory messages from alumni, friends, and students. One such telegram is typical: "The love devotion and loyalty of hundreds of your former students go out to you at this bitter hour." But he also got hate mail. One such letter was addressed to him as "Prof. of Bigotry," with the message, "Now just stop calumniating your brethren and broaden out your miserable theology and learn to be a Christian or else get out." Truly, Machen was experiencing his bitter hour.

His response, however, is noteworthy. He kept teaching and kept preaching—practically every Sunday and not only around Princeton, but also in Montreal and Toronto, St. Louis and Chicago. He kept writing for publication and also wrote letters to his former students, rejoicing in their ministries and taking great solace in their concern and sympathies for him. One alumnus had heard that Machen was ousted from Princeton in 1926 and offered his condolences and encouraged him to continue to "lead our thought in the line of the true and tried faith." Machen wrote back to correct the record, but also shared how, "despite these bitter experiences," the work of the Princeton alumni had made his life and effort worthwhile. He closed with these words: "Let me say again how deeply grateful I am to you for your letter, both because of the way in which you speak of me personally and also because of your devotion to the faith for the defense of which Princeton has always stood." What Machen may not have fully realized was that the strong stand of Princeton was beginning to waver.

A strategy was employed to wrest control of the seminary from conservatives by a seemingly innocuous merging of the two boards of the seminary. From its charter, Princeton had been governed by a board of directors that oversaw the educational enterprise and a board of trustees largely tasked with financial issues. At the time of the mid-1920s, the makeup of the two boards happened to be a cluster of conservatives on the board of directors and liberals or moderates on the board of trustees. The merger would effectively shift power from a conservative base to a moderate or liberal one. Machen, other faculty members, board members, alumni, and students protested, but to no avail. The plan for the merger—championed by the president of the seminary, J. Ross Stevenson, encouraged by Erdman, and approved by a number of folks in key positions in the denomination— prevailed, and the reorganization of Princeton Seminary came about at the close of the school year in 1929. The report of the incident, from the side of Stevenson, blamed Machen for the bad press brought to Princeton because of Machen's pernicious character and inflexible dogmatism. The cool and mollifying personality of Erdman was much preferred. In short, an effort was made to turn the controversy on issues of personality and not on issues of doctrine.

There is, however, another side. Perhaps Robert Dick Wilson, professor of Old Testament, saw the situation aright when he observed that it was a doctrinal issue, "the doctrine of the importance of doctrine."

Wilson's acuity in the matter had little bearing on the outcome. The "Old Princeton," which Machen viewed as having ended on the day of Warfield's funeral, finally succumbed. Machen's diary entry on May 3, 1929, records that he gave an exam and then attended a faculty meeting at 2:00, some of the last official duties of his twenty-two-year career at Princeton Theological Seminary. Machen no longer fit at the institution he had come to love, fight for, and so closely identify with. While not fired, he was left no real choice but to resign. But Machen did not give up on his calling to educate ministers and servants for the church. Having some financial means and a close-knit circle of supporters, Machen launched Westminster Theological Seminary in Philadelphia in 1929.

These had to be good days for Machen, especially given the struggles over the last five years. Gone were the politics that had infiltrated Princeton Seminary and soured his relationships with the administration and fellow faculty. At Westminster, all were knit together in their theology, philosophy of education, and vision of ministry. Machen often spoke of the seminary community as "our little company." With a distinct sense of carrying on the tradition of Old Princeton, Machen and his allies set about their task with firm resolve. He even mimicked Old Princeton's organizational scheme by not having a president. Instead, the seminary was run by a faculty committee, with Machen leading, of course, as Hodge and Warfield had been the titular head at Princeton.

And Machen was writing again. In 1930, his efforts would result in the publication of *The Virgin Birth of Christ,*

the standard scholarly defense of this crucial, orthodox doctrine for decades to come. As Machen declared in his opening address for Westminster Seminary, "No, my friends,
though Princeton Seminary is dead, the noble tradition of
Princeton Seminary is alive." That tradition, complete with
its dual commitment to scholarship and the church, was indeed alive. The seminary officially opened on September 25,
1929. Within one month, on October 24, Wall Street plum-
meted and the nation entered the Great Depression. On the
national front, the Roaring Twenties had come to an end
and new realities set in.

Machen was not yet past his hardships, either. In the next
few years, more conflict would come. Despite the fact that
some of it emanated from the seminary, Westminster remained for him a respite amid the rolling waves of conflict.

_3_

FINAL CONFLICTS, NEW BEGINNINGS
_1930–1937_

He stood for something and everyone knew what it was.

Pearl S. Buck, _"Tribute to Dr. Machen"_
The New Republic, _January 20, 1937_

Machen did not leave Princeton by himself; he was joined by Robert Dick Wilson and Oswald T. Allis in Old Testament and Cornelius Van Til in apologetics, with John Murray in systematic theology coming the following year. Three other Princeton alumni joined the faculty: Allen MacRae, Paul Woolley, and Ned Stonehouse. Stonehouse had studied New Testament at Princeton under Machen and had just earned his Ph.D. from the Free University of Amsterdam. Machen welcomed his assistance in New Testament, and the two forged a deep and abiding friendship. The new student body also consisted of those who had begun at Princeton and finished under Machen at Westminster. The first classes, though small, were impressive. They included J. Oliver Buswell, future president of Wheaton; Harold John Ockenga, future president of Fuller Seminary and Gordon-Conwell Seminary; and the colorful Carl McIntire. Even board members resigned their seats at Princeton to take them up at Westminster. Most notable among them is Samuel Craig.

Craig, educated at Princeton, had served two pastorates before taking on the duties of editor of *The Presbyterian,* an independent magazine that championed the conservative cause in the denomination. Machen contributed a number of articles and found a welcome ally in Craig. Because of his support of Machen through the Princeton controversy, Craig was fired as editor. Not to be thwarted, he, along with Machen and another Westminster board member, established *Christianity Today,* to carry on the mission of *The Presbyterian.* That same year in 1930 Craig also founded Presbyterian and Reformed Publishing Company. A few years later, Craig and Machen were to have a falling-out, but through these years, Craig's friendship and contribution meant a great deal to Machen.

Not everything, however, was so blissful. William Park Armstrong, Geerhardus Vos, and Caspar Wistar Hodge decided to remain at Princeton. All three did so reluctantly, however, and while they were not with Machen physically, they certainly were with him and his efforts in spirit. Even though Machen understood the reasoning of each one for staying behind, he was saddened that they did not take the courageous step with him. He nevertheless remained friends, corresponding frequently and visiting often. Additionally, while Machen was free from the controversy that had dogged him at Princeton, his battles in his denomination were only beginning.

All of this paled to the grief he encountered on the death of his mother on October 13, 1931. She was his biggest fan, her devotion unquestionable. She kept scrapbooks of his ac-

MAR.

FORUM
and Century

Woodrow Wilson After Ten Years
A Critical Appraisal of the War President   HAROLD J. LASKI

Those Misunderstood Puritans
And Their Legacy to Our Generation   SAMUEL ELIOT MORISON

Making War on the Gangs
A Plan to Take the Police out of Politics   SMEDLEY D. BUTLER

Christianity and Liberty
A Challenge to the "Modern Mind"   J. GRESHAM MACHEN

Wings of To-morrow
The Inventor of the Autogiro Looks at Aviation   JUAN DE LA CIERVA

Hard Times and Soft Thinking
A Critique of Our Business Leaders   FABIAN FRANKLIN

History's Greatest Dates
Results of The Forum's Prize Contest   THREE PRIZE WINNERS

25 CENTS
★

3.1. Machen's writings appeared in numerous venues beyond Christian publications, such as his article, "Christianity & Liberty," printed in *Forum and Century*, March, 1931.

complishments, complete with pictures and news clippings and letters from others commending her son. She had one devoted to his book *What Is Faith?* and one to *The Virgin Birth,* one on the Princeton controversy, and one on Westminster. She was working on a new one at the time of her death. In her last letter to her son, she voiced her unstinting support: "Mother is feeble, but she is with Dassie every step." She had counseled him through the vacillations of his youth, suffered with him through the tumultuous battles he endured, and rejoiced with him in his triumphs. Among their last correspondence was a number of letters on his book *The Virgin Birth*, a tour de force of scholarship. His mother pored over every line "with great profit and delight and a thankful pride in being uplifted and instructed by my own son." As Machen wrote on the day of her funeral, "My mother seems—to me at least—to have been the wisest and best human being I ever knew."

One final battle awaited Machen. In June 1933, frustrated by the presence of liberals working under the auspices of the Board of Foreign Missions, the denomination's mission agency, Machen and others organized the Independent Board of Foreign Missions. Machen was appointed president, and a board of ministers and ruling elders, as well as five women, was established. They all took this action to keep money out of the hands of liberal missionaries and direct it to those who would preach the gospel. As early as 1925, Machen, in a letter addressing his concerns over the mission board, expressed, "It is not now contrary to my conscience to give to our Foreign Board, though I can not say I give with much enthusiasm." By 1933, however, his conscience would no longer sustain mere apathy. At the center of his shift is the report, produced by a large group of laity with the support of the Presbyterian Church and six other denominations and funded by John D. Rockefeller, entitled *Re-Thinking Missions: A Laymen's Inquiry after One Hundred Years*. A quite early trove of pluralistic thought, the report advocated a paradigm shift in missions premised on the notion that Christianity is not the exclusively true religion.

Consequently, mission work should be more syncretistic, eschewing imperialistic attitudes about Christianity and proselytizing in favor of more accommodating attitudes toward other religions and their adherents. As Machen summed it up, the new task of missions was to seek the truth, not present it. The report inflamed the conservatives, and it also brought the simmering controversy in the Presbyterian Church to a full boil.

One of the report's champions was Presbyterian missionary to China and novelist Pearl S. Buck. Winning the Pulitzer Prize in 1932 for her novel *The Good Earth* and winning the Nobel Prize for literature in 1938, Buck had begun life as a child of missionaries in China. Later, she followed her parents, taking up the same work herself. Not only did she give a laudatory review of the report, claiming it as "the only book I ever read which seems to me literally true in its every observation," she also publicly rejected the deity of Christ, preferring instead to speak of him as "the essence of Men's highest dreams," and she discarded the need to preach the gospel—"I am weary unto death," she said, "with this incessant preaching." Machen responded with a 110-page work, *Modernism and the Board of Foreign Missions*. While not attacking Buck personally, Machen used the report and Buck's views to draw attention to the laxity that prevailed within the board, again driving home his point that the church suffered from an acute theological "indifferentism." And again headlines were made. Under protest, the mission board finally and reluctantly began a process of review of Buck and her views. She, however, relieved them of taking action by resigning, to which the board responded with regrets. Machen and the conservatives would have much preferred a more direct and swift response.

3.2. The faculty of Westminster Theological Seminary, c. 1930.   First row, from left: Ned B. Stonehouse, Oswald T. Allis, J. Gresham Machen, Paul Woolley, Cornelius Van Til. Second row: John Murray and Allan MacRae.

At the center of the soft-pedaling of the issue stood Robert Speer. Though opposed to the pluralistic tendency of *Re-Thinking Missions,* Speer actually wrote a rebuttal to such notions entitled *The Finality of Christ* (1933), and as secretary of the Board of Foreign Missions he followed a policy of mollification and tolerance. Speer and Machen had a history. Speer was on the board of trustees at Princeton and favored the plan for reorganization, his logic being that the seminary should represent all the views of the denomination and not simply reflect the more conservative elements. Speer was also a close ally and backer of Erdman. Machen pursued the present issue by filing an overture in his presbytery, the New Brunswick

Presbytery. Machen proposed four points. The first two follow in full:

1. To take care to elect to positions on the Board of Foreign Missions only persons who are fully aware of the danger in which the church stands and who are determined to insist upon such verities as the full truthfulness of Scripture, the virgin birth of our Lord, His substitutionary death as a sacrifice to satisfy Divine justice, His bodily resurrection and His miracles, as being essential to the Word of God and our Standards and as being necessary to the message which every missionary under our church shall proclaim.

2. To instruct the Board of Foreign Missions that no one who denies the absolute necessity of acceptance of such verities by every candidate for the ministry can possibly be regarded as competent to occupy the position of Candidate Secretary.

As a result of Machen's overture, the New Brunswick Presbytery brought Speer to its April meeting for what was supposed to be a debate with Machen. In the words of D. G. Hart, the contest "fizzled," with Machen being accused of "nitpicking," while Speer was lauded for taking the high road of Christian unity. "Not by suspicion and strife," Speer affably responded, "but by confidence and concord is the great work of our Redeemer to be done in the world by us who love Him."

In a clever debate tactic, Speer further turned Machen's points into mere fears of what might happen, and then argued that the potential gain was far greater than any dangers. He even played the patriotic card, referring to his great-great-grandfather's vote for the Constitution of the

United States, "in the face of the opposition of his constituents who feared the great dangers that lurked in the American union." This, of course, had nothing whatsoever to do with the issue at hand. It proved persuasive, nevertheless. Speer's victory ensured, the overture was defeated, and Speer and the Board of Foreign Missions were affirmed. The motion, however, passed in the Philadelphia Presbytery, largely due to the efforts of Clarence Macartney, thus securing a place on the docket for the 1933 General Assembly. There it met with defeat, however. Machen, along with others, announced in the summer of 1933 the formation of the Independent Board of Foreign Missions, "to promote truly Biblical and truly Presbyterian mission work."

The next year's General Assembly of the Presbyterian Church in the U.S.A. once again had Machen on the agenda. It declared the Independent Board unconstitutional, issued a cease-and-desist order, and called for discipline of anyone associated with it. The Independent Board was taken as an affront to the church and a violation of the ordination vows of its board members and missionaries. The Independent Board also caused consternation within the ranks of the conservatives, even hitting as close to home for Machen as Westminster Seminary. Oswald T. Allis and Samuel Craig broke off with Machen, as did Clarence Macartney of Arch Street Presbyterian Church in Philadelphia. Those who stuck with him faced discipline, endured church trials in their presbyteries, and were eventually stripped of their ministerial credentials.

This action, the establishing of the board, is probably one of the most difficult events of Machen's life to interpret. On the one hand, his action is consistent with his life and his commitment to the true gospel, no matter what the cost. On the other hand, it may not have been the wisest way to

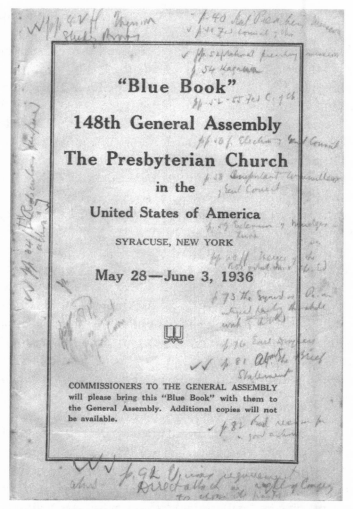

3.3. Machen's personal copy of the 1936 General Assembly "Blue Book." His handwritten notes fill the cover.

break from the church, or the most judicious move for the sake of the new seminary. At the least, it certainly was not in keeping with Presbyterian polity. On a more personal level, for Machen it caused a rift among some of his closest confidants and supporters. Of course, relationships with those who were with Machen, such as the young faculty members at Westminster, were deepened through the ordeal. Machen, however, felt hamstrung by the denomination, seeing the formation of the Independent Board, and sticking with it, as his only option.

Because of the General Assembly's action in 1934 declaring the new mission board unconstitutional, Machen and associates were plagued by church trials throughout the next two years. On March 29, 1935, making front-page news in *The New York Times*—"Presbytery to Try Machen as Rebel," ran the headline—Machen was officially defrocked and stripped of his credentials. Again, Machen's response in the face of defeat is noteworthy. Within months, Machen and others met to lay the groundwork for a new church. First, there would be a marked appeal to the General Assembly, which would not meet again until 1936. In late 1935, Machen and others also founded a new publication, *The Presbyterian Guardian,* to support both the seminary and the conservative cause. Machen busied himself writing for it and playing a leading role in editing and publishing it. The load of it all wearied him.

In the interim, and well in need of a rest, Machen took what was to be his last transatlantic voyage for an extensive vacation in 1935. Sailing for France, Machen left New York City on June 29. Though no longer able to write home to his parents, surely his thoughts turned to them as he toured the museums and galleries and stood breathless before the grandeur of the mountains. After a well-deserved rest, he returned. As he had done on his other trips, he made new acquaintances. For two evenings he played chess with a Mr. Lynn before the voyage came to an end and the ship docked at New York City's harbor. He preached at Boston in Park Street Church and then returned to Philadelphia to start another new school year. Ever since his early childhood, the fall months had found Machen in the company of academics. This school year, however, his main energies would be directed elsewhere as he geared up for the General Assembly and the inevitable outcome.

The General Assembly of 1936, meeting in Syracuse, New York, rejected the appeal of Machen and his compatriots. Not only did Machen have his own trial to contend with, but he also supported and counseled others, even paying legal fees to aid some of his former students in trials in their respective presbyteries. As Machen had not given up on his vocation of training ministers when he found himself at odds with Princeton Seminary, when ousted from his denomination he did not give up on his desire for a "truly Presbyterian church," as he often said. In her rather conciliatory obituary that would be written in January 1937, Pearl S. Buck cleverly summed it up: "I was kicked out of the back door of the church and he was kicked out of the front one. He retaliated by establishing a church of his own."

Consequently, wasting no time, on June 11, 1936, Machen led the First General Assembly of the new church, first named the Presbyterian Church of America, then renamed the Orthodox Presbyterian Church in 1939, as a result of a suit filed by the Presbyterian Church in the U.S.A. A rather small band, numbering only 120, declared, "We, a company of ministers and ruling elders, having been removed from [the Presbyterian Church in the U.S.A.] in contravention (as we believe) of its constitution, or having severed our connection with that organization, or hereby solemnly declaring that we do sever our connection with it . . . do hereby associate ourselves together with all Christian people who do and will adhere to us, in a body to be known and styled as the Presbyterian Church of America."

Reflecting on the moment, Machen declared, "We became members, at last, of a true Presbyterian Church; we recovered, at last, true Christian fellowship. What a joyous moment it was! How the long years of struggle seemed to sink into nothingness compared with the joy and peace that filled our hearts." Soon, however, the euphoria gave way to the realities of organizing a new church.

The First General Assembly largely got the ball rolling for the second one held that same year on November 12–15. One significant decision made at the first assembly, however, concerned the right of local churches to own their property. This was a lesson that many in the new denomination had learned the hard way. When the ministers were defrocked by the Presbyterian Church in the U.S.A., not only did they lose their pensions, many of them were literally locked out of their churches. Even if the entire congregation sided with the minister against the denomination, it mattered none because the denomination owned the property and assets of the local church. That brave stand taken in 1936 was costly to many for more than just their reputations. But to Machen and the others it was well worth the cost. At the Second General Assembly, Machen, in his role as moderator, delivered the sermon entitled "Constraining Love," on 2 Corinthians 5:14–15. The sermon, coming just before they were to partake of the Lord's Supper, resounded with Machen's vision of the new church, as he declared, "What a privilege to carry the message of the cross, unshackled by compromising associations, to all the world! What a privilege to send it to foreign lands! What a privilege to proclaim it to the souls of people who sit in nominally Christian churches and starve for lack of the bread of life!" Little did the auditors know that it was to be his farewell address.

In December of 1936, Machen boarded a train to bolster the new church in North Dakota. It was to be his final trip.

Worn down to the point of exhaustion and hit with inclement weather, Machen contracted pneumonia and died on January 1, 1937. As with most events in Machen's life, his death garnered the attention of the newspapers. The eulogies praised Machen—not the least of them coming from the typewriter of the infamous H. L. Mencken of *The Baltimore Sun*. He praised Machen for the astute scholarship and sensibilities that set him apart from both the fundamentalists, of whom it could almost be said that Mencken made a career out of parodying, and the modernists, who, in Mencken's eyes, had made religion "hardly more than a row of hollow platitudes, as empty of psychological force and effect as so many nursery rhymes." But Machen stood above it all, like, as Mencken said, the Matterhorn. And then Mencken offered his final assessment: "He failed—but he was undoubtedly right."

Not all would agree with the first half of this last line. It all depends, of course, on the standard of measure that one uses. Given that Machen was marginalized and then forced from Princeton and from his denomination, Mencken is right. Given the trajectory of mainline denominations in America in the twentieth century and now into the twenty-first, Mencken is right on this count, too. Machen himself, however, might prefer different markers to assess his life. It is true that in many ways his efforts failed. In these new institutions, however, he also tasted success.

But for Machen, his success was ultimately measured by something not quite of this world. Of the final moments before his mother died, he wrote, "But the thing that I really longed to hear in the moment of her parting from me was that she had been bought by the precious blood of Christ." Similar last words came from him as well: "I am so thankful," he said in his telegram to John Murray, "for [the] active obedience of Christ. No hope without it." For Machen,

FIG. 3.4

Timeline of Machen's Life

July 28, 1881	Born in Baltimore, Maryland
January 4, 1896	Becomes a confessing member at Franklin Street Presbyterian Church
1898–1901	Attends Johns Hopkins University, B.S.
1901–02	Undertakes graduate studies at Johns Hopkins University and the University of Chicago
1902–05	Attends Princeton University, M.A., and Princeton Theological Seminary, B.D.
1905	Publishes first article, "New Testament Account of Birth of Jesus" in the *Princeton Theological Review*
1905–06	Undertakes graduate study at Marburg and Göttingen in Germany
1906–29	Serves on the faculty of Princeton Theological Seminary
June 23, 1914	Is ordained in the Presbyterian Church in the U.S.A.
1914–15	Publishes *A Rapid Survey of the Literature and History of New Testament Times*
May 3, 1915	Is inaugurated as assistant professor at Princeton Seminary. Delivers address "History and Faith"
December 19, 1915	Father, Arthur Webster Machen, dies
1918–19	Serves with YMCA in France during World War I
1921	Publishes *The Origin of Paul's Religion*
February 16, 1921	Mentor and Colleague B. B. Warfield dies
1921	Is awarded D.D., Hampden-Sydney College
1922	Publishes *A Brief Bible History: A Survey of the Old and New Testaments*
May 21, 1922	[Harry Emerson Fosdick preaches sermon, "Shall the Fundamentalists Win?"]
1923	Publishes *New Testament Greek for Beginners* and *Christianity and Liberalism*

1924	[Modernists sign Auburn Affirmation]
1925	Publishes *What Is Faith?*
1925	Ceases to be stated supply at First Presbyterian, Princeton, following controversy
1926	Is appointed chair of apologetics, not confirmed by General Assembly
1928	Is awarded Litt. D., Wheaton College
1929	Princeton Theological Seminary is reorganized
September 25, 1929	Opens Westminster Theological Seminary in Philadelphia
1930	Publishes *The Virgin Birth of Christ*
October 13, 1931	Mother, Mary Gresham Machen, dies
1933	[*Re-Thinking Missions: A Laymen's Inquiry after One Hundred Years* is released]
1933	Elected president of new Independent Board of Foreign Missions
March 29, 1935	Is declared guilty of violating ordination vows. Appeals to General Assembly
1936	Publishes *Christian Faith in the Modern World* (radio addresses on WIP, Philadelphia)
June 1936	His appeal to General Assembly is rejected; he is officially defrocked
June 11, 1936	Elected first moderator of new Presbyterian Church of America (changed name to Orthodox Presbyterian Church in 1939)
January 1, 1937	Dies in North Dakota; buried in Baltimore
1937	*The Christian View of Man* (his radio addresses on WIP, Philadelphia) is published
1949	*God Transcendent* (his collected sermons), edited by Ned B. Stonehouse, is published
1951	*What Is Christianity? And Other Addresses*, edited by Ned B. Stonehouse, is published

all—that is, all the battles, all the education, all the writing, all the efforts for the new seminary and the new church, and all the grief and all the joy—was for the gospel. Not surprisingly, Machen took Isaac Watts's "When I Survey the Wondrous Cross" as his favorite hymn. Machen quoted the hymn in his sermon that November at the Second General Assembly of the fledgling church. He then declared, "The overpowering love of Christ for us, manifested when he died for us on the cross, calls forth our all in response. Nothing can be so precious to us that we should not give it up to him who gave himself there for us on the tree." All the lines of that hymn paint the picture of Machen's life, but perhaps none so vividly as those in the second stanza:

> Forbid it, Lord, that I should boast,
> Save in the death of Christ, my God;
> All the vain things that charm me most,
> I sacrifice them to his blood.

Conclusion

Machen's driver's license application for 1919 gave the following details: "Date of birth July 28, 1881; color White; Height 5 ft. 8 in.; weight 150 lbs; sex Male; color of eyes Brown; color of hair Dark Brown." His extraordinary life and legacy belies his fairly average description. Because of his passion for long walks and vigorous exercise throughout his life, he stayed around his trim 150 pounds, although his weight went up a little toward the very end of his life—his crowded schedule left little time for his exercise routines. His days of mountain-climbing had passed, and he had exchanged the tree-lined streets of Princeton for the brownstones and budding high-rises of Philadelphia by the time of his death.

Yet even though it may have been slow in coming, his commitment to the rigorous defense of the Christian faith, to careful and responsible scholarship, and above all to the church of Jesus Christ never wavered. Though his life, from one vantage point, may seem to have been cut short, his legacy continues through his books, his students and the other lives he touched, and the institutions he founded. It is fittingly ironic that it takes one of his dissenters to get him best, as Pearl S. Buck offers the appropriate final word: "He stood for something and everyone knew what it was."

A Note on the Sources

Machen's voluminous letters and archives, including the Brooks Brothers receipt, are housed in the Montgomery Library, Westminster Theological Seminary. Additional archival material may be found at Speer Library, Princeton Theological Seminary. The classic biography of Machen is Ned B. Stonehouse, *J. Gresham Machen: A Biographical Memoir* (1954). The following are also quite helpful: D. G. Hart, *Defending the Faith: J. Gresham Machen and the Crisis of Conservative Protestantism in Modern America* (1994); Paul Woolley, *The Significance of J. Gresham Machen Today* (1977); and Henry W. Coray, *J. Gresham Machen: A Silhouette* (1981). For broader treatments of Machen and the fundamentalist/modernist controversy, see William R. Hutchison, *The Modernist Impulse in American Protestantism* (1992); Bradley Longfield, *The Presbyterian Controversy: Fundamentalists, Modernists, and Moderates* (1991); George M. Marsden, *Understanding Fundamentalism and Evangelicalism* (1991); and Edwin H. Rian, *The Presbyterian Conflict* (1992). For a history of Princeton Seminary, see David B. Calhoun, *Princeton Seminary* (1994–1996).

PART 2

MACHEN AS SCHOLAR: WRITINGS ON THEOLOGY AND THE BIBLE

The major books published by Machen in his lifetime remain in print. They not only spoke to the times when they were written, but continue to have something meaningful for today. In this section we explore four of these books, beginning with the classic *Christianity and Liberalism*. This book signaled Machen's career as a premier defender of orthodox theology and made him a spokesperson, if somewhat reluctantly, for fundamentalism during the modernist crisis in the church. The next chapter treats the sequel, *What Is Faith?* These two books accomplish far more than a response to liberalism, as they offer succinct and compelling presentations of the Christian view of the Bible, Christ, God, humanity, salvation, and faith. Chapter 6 treats the last two books examined in this section, *The Origin of Paul's Religion* and *The Virgin Birth of Christ*. Spanning a rather eventful decade, these two works reveal Machen's abilities as a New Testament scholar. In fact, here we see Machen going toe to toe with the most brilliant minds of the liberal position, dealing a decisive blow to the views that Paul invented Christianity by distorting Christ's teaching and that the virgin birth is the stuff of myth and legend. Machen counters with a sterling presentation of the central truths of Christianity.

4

An Admirable Book:
Christianity and Liberalism

If Jesus was only what the liberal historians suppose that He was, then trust in Him would be out of place.

J. *Gresham Machen,* Christianity and Liberalism

We shall do well to listen to Dr. Machen.

Walter Lippman

When diplomacy was called for, J. Gresham Machen used it, as in a letter to an unfortunate student in one of his New Testament exegesis classes at Princeton. The student's performance was "below the passing mark," a gentle means of communicating that he had failed. Diplomacy, however, needed to be set aside to answer liberalism. This was due not only to the exigencies of the matter, but also to the disingenuous writings from the liberal side. Christianity was being retooled, and the prophets of the new order were making subtle and, especially to the casual observer, seemingly innocuous revisions of Christianity in the process of making it more palatable for moderns. Machen could ill afford to use his words carelessly or even ambiguously. The stakes were too high, leaving him no option but to speak the truth, and to speak it bluntly. Liberalism, he simply and forcefully declared, is not Christianity, not even a faint version of it.

The immediate context of *Christianity and Liberalism* is the sermon preached by Harry Emerson Fosdick, "Shall the Fundamentalists Win?," on May 21, 1922, and the tempest of the fundamentalist/modernist controversy in America. Enjoying the favor of John D. Rockefeller, Fosdick's sermon was reprinted and widely distributed. The sermon brought forth a response by Machen's friend and Princeton alumnus Clarence Edward Noble Macartney. At the time, Macartney pastored Arch Street Presbyterian Church in Philadelphia. In 1924 he would be elected as moderator of the General Assembly, barely edging out Charles Erdman by a mere two-point spread. Though in the 1930s Macartney distanced himself from Machen, disagreeing with Machen's move to organize the Independent Board of Foreign Missions, in these early years the two were comrades in the fight against liberalism. Machen followed up Macartney's sermon with his own response, a book-length salvo, *Christianity and Liberalism*—by many accounts a theological classic.

Fosdick's sermon, however, provides only the immediate context. To fully grasp the weight of Machen's book, one must go back twenty years and travel a few thousand miles to Marburg, Germany, to the lectures of Wilhelm Herrmann during Machen's student days in 1905. Like Fosdick, Herrmann envisioned a Christianity that need not depend on the historical facts of the virgin birth and the resurrection. Unlike Fosdick's flowery, sentimental substitute, however, Herrmann's faith was palpable and vivid and deeply felt. So much so that Herrmann threw Machen into a quagmire, albeit only temporarily. His mentor and soon-to-be colleague at Princeton, William Park Armstrong, benefited as he was by his distance and safety in the environs of Princeton, saw through Herrmann's piety in a facile and speedy manner. Machen, closely connected as he was, hesitated. Is Christianity a *true* religion, in accordance with the facts of history, and therefore, because of that truthfulness, meaningful? Or does it become real and meaningful as it is borne out by experience?

Though hesitating, Machen never could concur with Herrmann, and as he returned from Germany he rejected wholesale Herrmann's revision of Christianity. When he found himself dealing with the same issues two decades later in the work of Fosdick, he did not hesitate in the least, quickly and forcefully declaring that the revision proposed by Fosdick and liberalism was not even a distant relative of Christianity. In fact, as the central thesis of the book resounds, liberalism is something different from Christianity altogether. In the pages that follow, we'll first examine Fosdick's sermon and then explore Machen's response. Yet, as is true with most of his works, Machen's response goes far beyond the contemporary situation and speaks to issues of timeless import.

An Explosion of Ill Will

It would be hard to calculate the number of sermons preached in America. Now into the fifth century of American preaching, the number of sermons has to be staggering. Yet among that number, only a few stand out as remarkable, epoch-making texts. And the ones that do usually do so accidentally. One such sermon is Fosdick's "Shall the Fundamentalists Win?" In his autobiography, written many years after he preached the sermon, Fosdick viewed it as a failure. While Machen would offer such a designation for a different reason, Fosdick reached this conclusion because what he intended as a herald of goodwill instead "was an explosion of ill will, for over two years making headline news of a controversy that went the limits of truculence." Examining the content of the sermon lends a certain naiveté to Fosdick's sense of what his sermon would accomplish. Not only does he gloss over significant differences on three crucial doctrines, he also vituperates—the word Machen preferred to describe the sermon's impact—fundamentalists and theological conservatives. A walk through the sermon bears this out.

Fosdick begins by drawing attention to the divisive fundamentalism looming on the landscape and signals the battle cry for tolerance and civility, the very qualities he deemed the fundamentalists to be lacking. In addition to labeling fundamentalists as "illiberal and intolerant," Fosdick further views them as backward thinkers, quite out of step with modernity. So he proposes both a more tolerant and a more modern approach. "We must," he declares, "be able to think

Fig. 4.1

"The Five Point Deliverance"

Scripture's Inspiration and Inerrancy

Christ's Virgin Birth

Christ's Substitutionary Atonement

Christ's Bodily Resurrection
(as an Historical Event)

Christ's Performance of Miracles
during His Earthly Ministry

"The Five Point Deliverance," popularly called "The Five Fundamentals," was passed by the Presbyterian General Assembly in 1910.

our modern life clear through in Christian terms, and to do that we must be able to think our Christian faith clear through in modern terms." He then shows exactly what he has in mind, listing the fundamental doctrines affirmed in the Five Point Deliverance at the 1910 General Assembly of the Presbyterian Church in the U.S.A., although he substituted the second coming of Christ for Christ's bodily resurrection. While Fosdick observes, "This is a free country and anyone has a right to hold these opinions," he has significant problems with anyone who would view them as binding for the church or as boundary markers of orthodoxy. In the bulk of the sermon, he takes up three of the so-called fundamentals of the faith: Christ's virgin birth, the inspiration and inerrancy of Scripture, and Christ's second coming.

A pattern emerges for his treatment of each of these doctrines. He first presents two perspectives on the doctrine—the conservative and the liberal, respectively—then argues that the church is big enough to make room for adherents of both. Consequently, when speaking of the virgin birth, he notes that the first view holds, "The virgin birth is to be accepted as historical fact; it actually happened; there was no other way for a personality like the Master to come into this world except by a special biological miracle." The other view is a little more complicated. Fosdick explains it this way: "To believe in virgin birth as an explanation of great personality is one of the familiar ways in which the ancient world was accustomed to account for unusual superiority."

He continues, observing that it is quite false to see Christ's virgin birth as unique. In fact, "According to the records of their faiths, Buddha and Zoroaster and Lao-Tsze and Mahavira were all supernaturally born," as were Plato and Augustus Caesar. The disciples, he reasons, thought so highly of Christ's special origin that they framed it as the virgin birth, concluding, "They phrased it in terms of a biological miracle that our modern minds cannot use." (This is what Fosdick has in mind when he speaks of thinking "our Christian faith clear through in modern terms.") He follows with the claim that "the Christian church [should be] large enough to hold within her hospitable fellowship people who differ on points like this." When he encounters the inerrancy and inspiration of the Bible and Christ's second coming, briefly tacking on Christ's atonement at the end, he follows exactly the same pattern.

He ends the sermon with two closing comments of application. First, he calls for "a spirit of tolerance and Christian liberty." Second, he exhorts the church to "penitent shame [for] quarreling over little matters when the world is dying of great needs." "It is almost unforgivable," he expounds, "that men should tithe mint and anise and cumin, and quarrel over them, when the world is perishing." In his reply, Macartney returned, "[Fosdick] thus likens the question of the virgin birth, the inspiration of the Bible, the second advent of Christ, and the atonement to mint, anise, and cumin. To me, this seems an almost unpardonable flippancy on the part of one who speaks as a teacher of Christianity." Over doctrinal verity and precision, Fosdick preferred personal piety and devotion and tolerance. Both Macartney and Machen, following Fosdick's lead about this being a free country, grant that Fosdick is entitled to his views on these issues. Only, they argue, he has no warrant to call them Christian.

A Time of Conflict

The firestorm set off by his sermon might very well have come as a surprise to Fosdick. Given the nature of his revision of Christian doctrines, however, to anyone with a modicum of knowledge of orthodox Christianity it is no surprise at all that the sermon only fanned the flames of the controversy. As Machen writes in his book, "The present time is a time of conflict." To Machen, these differences are not trifles over peripheral doctrines, and this was not the time for civility and tolerance. As Machen reflects on Fosdick's views, however, he finds something equally troubling as Fosdick's conclusions, namely, the reasoning Fosdick used to get there. Fosdick preferred devotion and piety over doctrinal accuracy; what mattered was being a "devoted lover of the Lord," not having right doctrine. This stumped Machen. Not because he was against piety or against devotion, but because Fosdick's view left him with too many nagging questions. If Christ is not virgin-born and he is not to be taken as the Bible presents him, then who exactly is it that one is to be a lover of in Fosdick's view? And if his death was not a sacrifice to remove the penalty and consequent judgment of sin, then what exactly was Christ doing on the cross? When Fosdick brushed aside doctrine for piety, he was not talking about tertiary issues; he was obliterating the very center of Christianity.

This same dynamic troubled Machen when he considered the moderate response to liberalism. The logic of the moderate was that the liberal's heart was right, that there was value to be gained from his perspective. Machen's response was that a Christianity not built on orthodox doctrine was living on borrowed time, verging on becoming mere moralism. Macartney concurred, offering the following assessment: "The movement is slowly secularizing the church and, if permitted to go unchecked and unchallenged, will ere long produce in our churches a new kind of Christianity, a Christianity of opinions and principles and good purposes, but a Christianity without worship, without God, and without Jesus Christ." His words presaged the famous statement by H. Richard Niebuhr summarizing liberalism: "A God without wrath brought men without sin into a kingdom without judgment through the ministrations of a Christ without a cross." In *Christianity and Liberalism,* Machen put it succinctly: Christianity is a doctrine, not a lifestyle. At first glance, Machen's dictum more than likely runs counter to contemporary evangelical sensibilities, and even, some might argue, runs counter to biblical Christianity. But his statement calls for more than a first glance; it compels a deeper look.

In the first chapter, Machen argues that there are two separate systems vying for the church: "the great redemptive religion which has always been known as Christianity," on the one hand, and, on the other, "a totally diverse type of religious belief, which is only the more destructive of the Christian faith because it makes use of traditional Christian terminology." This is modernism or liberalism, both terms being, according to Machen, "unsatisfactory; the latter, in particular is question-begging. The movement designated as 'liberalism' is regarded as 'liberal' only by its friends; to its opponents it seems to involve a narrow ignoring of many relevant facts." Machen also questions that the movement is modern. He makes the case that it responds to the challenge of modernity, one element of which is the ascendancy of the natural sciences as the arbiter of truth, by dodging the scientific question altogether and making Christianity true based on experience, or the sheer force of willing it to be true. Ironically, it is the conservative position, founded as it is on matters of fact and history, that is actually more scientific, whereas the liberal view is, as Machen argues, "unscientific." What ultimately matters, however, is that the liberal view is "un-Christian."

It's about Doctrine

Consequently, Machen intends to show in the chapters that follow that "despite the use of traditional phraseology modern liberalism not only is a different religion from Christianity but belongs in a totally different class." What Machen means is that Christianity (as he learned most forcefully from Warfield) is at bottom supernatural, while liberalism in its elevation of humanity and concomitant lowering of Christ is at bottom a natural religion. He makes his argument in the next six chapters of the book first by looking at the nature of doctrine and then by specifically examining the doctrines of God and humanity, the Bible, Christ, salvation, and the church. Machen offers a most provocative thesis in chapter 2 concerning the nature of doctrine. Contrary to the liberal point of view, which holds that Christianity is a lifestyle, Machen argues that Christianity is a doctrine. He nuances his view by adding that it is, indeed, also a lifestyle, but quickly adds that it is one founded on and necessarily preceded by doctrine.

To make his point, he turns to Christian origins, noting, "The Christian movement at its inception was not just a way of life in the modern sense, but a way of life founded upon a message. It was based, not upon mere feeling, not upon a mere program of work, but on an account of facts. In other words, it was based upon doctrine." This was true of the gospel writers and of Paul—the latter being no stranger to Machen, having just written *The Origins of Paul's Religion*. Machen observes, "Paul was convinced of the objective truth of the gospel message, and devotion to that truth was the great passion of his life." Machen bases this observation on 1 Corinthians 15, which he sees as encapsulating the very center of Christianity. Machen captures the essence of Paul's summary of the gospel in the early verses of that chapter when he writes, " 'Christ died'—that is history; 'Christ died for our sins'—that is doctrine. Without these two elements, joined in absolutely indissoluble union, there is no Christianity." The work of Christ in history provides the only sure basis for salvation, the truth of which the church has been called to bear witness. "Not to inner spiritual facts," Machen concludes, "but to what Jesus had done once for all in his death and resurrection."

Machen, however, entertains the liberal response that asks whether it is not possible to somehow see in Christ certain spiritual truths and trust in those, however vague they might be, for salvation. He follows with a response that such a designation is not trust but merely admiration or reverence. He continues, "They reverence Jesus as the supreme Person of all history and the supreme revealer of God. But trust can come only when the supreme Person extends his saving power *to us.* 'He went about doing good,' 'He spake words such as never man spake,' 'He is the express image of God'—that is reverence; 'He loved me and gave himself for me'—that is faith." Vacating Christ of his specific work in accomplishing salvation in history leaves him less than a Savior, and any religion that proposes such a position, according to Machen, leaves it less than Christianity. Machen, however, is just getting started. He continues to drive his point home by examining specific doctrines, beginning with a look at the doctrines of God and of humanity together.

One of the catchphrases of liberalism that emerged quite early on is "the fatherhood of God, the brotherhood of man," revealing the fundamental belief in the universal fatherhood of God. This perplexes Machen, precisely because he does not see Jesus teaching such a notion. To be sure, God is the creator of all and, through his work of common grace, cares for and even provides good things for all. As both Christ and the New Testament authors used the term, however, God as Father applies distinctly "to the company of the redeemed." The slogan of liberalism is only a symptom of the true problem in terms of liberalism's view of both God and human beings.

FIG. 4.2

Significant Events in the Fundamentalist/Modernist Controversy

1910	Presbyterian General Assembly requires affirmation of Five Point Deliverance for ordination
1910–15	*The Fundamentals* published
May 21, 1922	Harry Emerson Fosdick, "Shall the Fundamentalists Win?"
July 1922	Clarence Edward Macartney, "Shall Unbelief Win? A Response to Harry Emerson Fosdick"
1923	J. Gresham Machen, *Christianity and Liberalism*
1924	Auburn Affirmation
1924	Shailer Mathews, *The Faith of Modernism*
July 1925	Scopes Monkey Trial, Dayton, Tennessee
1925	J. Gresham Machen, *What Is Faith?*
1927	Presbyterian General Assembly rescinds affirmation of Five Point Deliverance for ordination

An inverse relationship emerges whenever one considers God and humans. That is to say, if one thinks quite highly of God, then it is quite natural also to think lowly of human beings. If, however, one thinks quite highly of human beings, their abilities, and their innate goodness, then one thinks lesser of God. Machen explains it this way, in view of the doctrine of the transcendence of God: "From beginning to end the Bible is concerned to set forth the great gulf that separates creature from Creator." When that great divide is glossed over, however, one loses sight of both the majesty of God and the frailty and dependence and sinfulness of the creature. Machen explores different reasons why the sense of sin no longer pervades humanity's thoughts as it once might have. He concludes that it has to do with the emphasis, prevalent in modern culture, on "unaided human nature." This, according to Machen, also prevailed in the church, as he observes, "Modern preachers are trying to bring men into the church without requiring them to relinquish their pride; they are trying to help men avoid the conviction of sin." Consequently, the church "is busily engaged in an absolutely impossible task—she is busily engaged in calling the righteous to repentance."

In his sermon, one of the three main issues that Fosdick challenged was the inerrancy and inspiration of the Bible. He presented the liberal view as inspiring, as opposed to inspired. It looked to the living word of God in humanity's progress or in Christian experience, as opposed to the spoken Word in the Bible. Machen counters by declaring, "The Christian man, on the other hand, finds in the Bible the very Word of God." In fact, Machen observes that this difference is foundational and therefore goes a long way in explaining how liberalism and Christianity are so totally different from one another. One of the clearest differences, in addition to those already sketched, regards Christ.

The Fairest Flower of Humanity

In perhaps some of the most crucial paragraphs of the book, Machen contends, "If Jesus was only what the liberal historians suppose that He was, then trust in Him would be out of place. . . . But if He was what the New Testament represents Him as being, then we can safely commit to Him the eternal destinies of our souls." He asks what the difference is between the perspectives, answering that "liberalism regards Jesus as the fairest flower of humanity; Christianity regards Him as a supernatural Person." He emphasizes *supernatural* not only to capture the deity of Christ, but also to draw attention to the miracles that Christ performed. Liberalism rejected the New Testament accounts of such miracles, seeing them as the result of fanciful imaginations or as merely mythical ways to express some sense of Christ's uniqueness or superiority. In fact, liberalism's rejection of believing in miracles stemmed from the denial of his deity, the denial that he was in fact a supernatural person. Machen puts it this way: "The question concerning all miracles is simply the question of the acceptance or the rejection of the Saviour that the New Testament presents." Jesus, according to Machen, in the liberal view ends up being different in degree; in the biblical view, he is also different in kind. At one point, Machen comments that Christianity has one distinct advantage over liberalism in reference to Christ: the Christ of Christianity is real.

A difference in the view of the work of Christ naturally follows from the difference outlined in the view of the person of Christ. Consequently, in the next chapter Machen turns to salvation, summing up the difference here by noting that liberalism finds "salvation (so far as it is willing to speak at all of 'salvation') in man; Christianity finds it in an act of God." This chapter in his book essentially deals with the implication of the issues explored in the previous ones. Given that God, humanity, the Bible, and the person of Christ are all diminished in liberalism, it follows that liberalism would have only an anemic salvation to offer. The particular issue at hand concerns the doctrine of the atonement. In liberalism, Christ's work on the cross becomes a symbol of the selfless act of sacrifice. In Christianity, the work of Christ on the cross is quite literally the lifeblood of the Christian. Turning to his favorite hymn, as he often did, Machen sees Isaac Watts's "When I Survey the Wondrous Cross" as perfectly capturing what Christ accomplished on the cross and the only possible way in which one could respond. He weaves a number of threads in his book together when he exclaims, "When we come to see that it was no mere man who suffered on Calvary but the Lord of Glory, then we shall be willing to say that one drop of the precious blood of Jesus is of more value, for our own salvation and the hope of society, than all the rivers of blood that have flowed upon the battlefields of history." His language points to the power of the vicarious sacrifice of Christ on the cross to pay for our sins.

In addition to treating Christ's atonement, Machen takes up in this chapter, and also in the next one on the church, the different views of liberalism and Christianity on the church's role in society. He raises all the great challenges of his day: the issue of industrialization, of world peace in the wake of World War I, of immigrants, and of the encroachment of Bolshevism. Machen recognizes that salvation and Christianity, while dealing with individual sin, do have something to say to these social issues. But—and here is the crucial difference—in liberalism all is reduced to the treatment of the social issues. This does not mean that the Christian avoids engagement of social issues. On the contrary, Machen argues, "The 'otherworldliness' of Christianity involves no withdrawal from the battle of this world; our Lord Himself, with his stupendous mission, lived in the midst of life's throng and press. Plainly, then, the Christian man may not simplify his problem by withdrawing from the business of the world, but must learn to apply the principles of Jesus even to the complex problems of modern industrial life." The difference is that for the Christian, this is the application of Christianity, whereas for the liberal, this is Christianity. And, Machen contends, "that difference makes itself felt everywhere."

It appears most significantly in the nature of the church, Machen's final chapter. Liberalism has posed perhaps its most significant problem by redefining the church as the "brotherhood of man," and not maintaining the biblical definition of a company of the redeemed. Consequently, "The greatest menace to the Christian Church to-day comes not from the enemies outside, but from the enemies within." Machen is not presuming to possess some mystical quality that allows him to see the true state of individual souls. Instead, he is pointing to those who knowingly and admittedly confess a different religion from Christianity, those who deny the very doctrines he's been discussing in the book. The only hope, as Machen sees it, to which he refers as "the crying need of the hour," is for "a separation between the two parties in the Church." As Machen has argued, Christianity is one thing, liberalism another. And the church can ill afford not to see the difference.

Conclusion

Machen's *Christianity and Liberalism* has become a classic. For some, it is read as a historical curiosity, offering insight into an intriguing religious and cultural debate in American history. For others, it is taken more seriously as a guide, a true help in responding to the perennial problems that the book addresses. Ralph Waldo Emerson once said of John Brown, "We meet him wherever we turn." So it is with Fosdick and his views. Fosdick's sermon became so popular because what he said appeals. Liberalism became so prominent because it charms, perhaps even beguiles. This should not surprise anyone. Before one even gets out of the pages of the New Testament, one is confronted with those who, using the language of the church, are proffering a different gospel. And today, there are manifestations of Fosdick and the same arguments he made as well. Like John Brown, we still meet him. But thankfully, we also still meet Machen, and the force of his arguments still remains.

In 1923, the book was not a classic. In fact, in its first year it sold only 1,000 copies. But then it got reviewed. The reviews were not always positive, though the negative ones boosted sales. As Machen pointed out in a letter to Andrew Rule, a professor at Illinois College who was using Machen's book as a text, "The tirade by Nolan Best in *The Continent* helped greatly in the sale of the book." In 1924 sales increased to 5,000 and have remained brisk since—enough, at least, for the book to have stayed in print eighty years later. Beyond the reviews' helping sales, Machen was also interested in their nature. He was especially interested in a piece published in *The Pacific Unitarian,* observing, "It shows how much more clearly Unitarians can (or rather will) get the point than those who are trying to justify to themselves and others their absolutely untenable position in the creedal churches." The Pulitzer Prize–winning journalist, author, and culture critic Walter Lippman had this to say: "It is an admirable book. For its acumen, for its saliency, and for its wit, this cool and stringent defense of orthodox Protestantism is, I think, the best popular argument produced by either side in the controversy. We shall do well to listen to Dr. Machen. The liberals have yet to answer him."

Those outside the church got Machen's point, but for those inside it was a different matter. As can be expected, the reviews from the liberal side, while castigating the book, dodged the substantive issues Machen had raised. Equally intriguing are the comments by his colleagues at Princeton Seminary. J. Ross Stevenson, the seminary's president and a good representative of the moderate position, largely hailed the book in a personal congratulatory letter to Machen. But he, according to Machen, went on to express "the view that we should not stir up trouble by cutting the liberals out of the church, but should let them remain in the church and should try to win them!" Missing Machen's point in the book entirely, Stevenson failed to realize the danger of the liberal element present in the church. Evangelizing liberals was one thing, at least to Machen, but giving them a continued foothold in the church was something altogether different.

Of course, Stevenson's remarks were driven by his sense of unity, the same litmus test that Fosdick used. In fact, the cry for unity was the practically reflexive criticism hurled at the work of the theological conservatives from all sides. But Machen, using Wilson's World War I slogan, saw that what the moderates and liberals wanted was "peace without victory." To this, Machen responded, "Mere concessiveness, therefore, will never succeed in avoiding the intellectual conflict." Machen wanted unity, the genuine unity of fellow believers, anchored in their union with Christ. Machen closed the earlier referenced letter to Andrew Rule with this observation: "We are in a great fight, and we are fighting, I am convinced, for the unity of the church, not against it. The only trouble is that the fight ought to have been made twenty years ago before the disintegrating elements had become so powerful."

Machen's book galvanized the conservatives, providing them with a place to stand. Despite its lucidity, however, his eleventh-hour attempt to stop the theological slide prevailed little in the fundamentalist/modernist controversy in the Presbyterian Church in the U.S.A. and in the broader circles of American Christianity. That by no means discredits the book or marks it a failure. In fact, the outcome of that debate proves Machen's observation that Christianity not founded on orthodox doctrine is living on borrowed time. He reminds us that in order for there to be any truly vital Christianity, it must be built on a solid foundation of doctrine.

It's fitting that Machen ends his book by discussing the church. In the last few paragraphs he paints a picture of a soul "weary with the conflicts of the world" entering "the church to seek refreshment," only to find that "the preacher comes forward, not out of a secret place of meditation and power, not with the authority of God's Word permeating his message, not with human wisdom pushed far into the background by the glory of the Cross, but with human opinions about the social problems of the hour or easy solutions of the vast problem of sin." Machen laments, "Sad indeed is the heart of the man who has come seeking peace." Alternatively, Machen offers a vision of a church founded on doctrine, gathered in fellowship and in union with Christ, and living "in sole reliance upon the Saviour who bought us with his blood." "And," he concludes, "from under the threshold of that house will go forth a river that will revive the weary world."

A Note on the Sources

Harry Emerson Fosdick's sermon has been anthologized numerous times, recently appearing in *American Sermons: The Pilgrims to Martin Luther King, Jr.,* edited by Michael Warner (1999), 775–86. Clarence Macartney's sermon "Shall Unbelief Win? An Answer to Dr. Fosdick" is reprinted in *Sermons That Shaped America: Reformed Preaching from 1630 to 2001,* edited by William S. Barker and Samuel T. Logan Jr. (2003), 323–43. Machen's *Christianity and Liberalism* is reprinted by Eerdmans (most recently, 2002). For specific treatments of Fosdick and of *Christianity and Liberalism,* see Bradley Longfield, *The Presbyterian Controversy* (1991), 9–27; D. G. Hart, *Defending the Faith* (1994), 59–83; and Ned B. Stonehouse, *J. Gresham Machen* (1987), 335–50. For a discussion of Wilhelm Herrmann and German liberalism, see Hendrikus Berkhof, *Two Hundred Years of Theology: Report of a Personal Journey* (1989); for a broad discussion of liberalism in America, see William R. Hutchison, *The Modernist Impulse in American Protestantism* (1992).

5

DEFENDER OF THE FAITH: *WHAT IS FAITH?*

"What is Faith?" A more "practical" question could hardly be conceived.

Salvation does not depend upon the strength of our faith, but it depends on Christ.

J. Gresham Machen, What Is Faith?

Ned B. Stonehouse, Machen's able biographer, referred to it as a sequel to the penetrating and insightful *Christianity and Liberalism.* The liberal response to it, from both scholar and pastor alike, castigated it, though not to anyone's, especially Machen's, surprise. Quite unexpectedly, *The British Weekly,* in no fewer than eight separate reviews, by and large hailed it, commending what was now referred to as Machen's characteristic scholarship, acuity, and forceful expression. It was his fourth book, entitled *What Is Faith?,* published by Macmillan in the fall of 1925.

The Clash of the Titans: The Battle over Liberalism

In the years surrounding 1923's publication of *Christianity and Liberalism,* life proved full and busy for Professor Machen. The year of 1925 was no exception. On the national front, all eyes were turned toward Dayton, Tennessee, and the clash of the titans William Jennings Bryan, Clarence Darrow, and H. L. Mencken—all clamoring over a rather hapless science teacher, John T. Scopes, who had violated Tennessee state law by teaching Darwin's theory of natural selection. Capturing front-page headlines, the Scopes Monkey Trial, the first case to be termed "The Trial of the Century," raged all through the summer, fueled by the Tennessee heat.

Earlier in the year, on March 1, Machen's stint as stated supply at the First Presbyterian Church of Princeton had come to an end, largely because of his clash with a titan of a different sort, Henry van Dyke. Van Dyke had been minister at the prestigious Brick Presbyterian Church in New York City. Through his writings, especially his tale *The Other Wise Man,* van Dyke won an appointment as professor of literature at Princeton University, a post he held only with the interruption of serving as ambassador to Luxembourg and the Netherlands, having been appointed by his friend President Woodrow Wilson. Shortly after Machen ascended the pulpit at First Presbyterian, van Dyke abandoned his pew. When Machen stepped down, replaced by seminary colleague Charles Erdman, van Dyke returned to his pew. Both events were made quite public with notices appearing in *The New York Times.* What Machen did not realize at the time was that these were merely skirmishes, foreshadowing the battle that would occupy him for the next decade.

In the summer of 1925, while William Jennings Bryan was fighting tooth and nail on what he thought to be the true front in the war between liberalism and Christianity at

Dayton, Machen was quietly lecturing at the Grove City Bible Conference. Machen, along with many others, had been invited by Bryan to appear as an expert witness for the prosecution. He declined, ostensibly citing his lack of expertise. Perhaps the real reason lies elsewhere. For Machen, while he did not discredit Bryan's work, the creation-versus-evolution controversy was not the decisive battle with liberalism. He saw it lying elsewhere.

Defining liberalism is tricky. So many centers of thought and disparate figures claim the label that summarizing and narrowly defining it can be a rather difficult task. Yet there are certain elements that one can latch on to. One of these has to do with the question of authority. Simply put, liberalism rejects the authority of the Bible, placing authority in human reason. Applied in the case of evolution versus creation, the result is that science, as understood from the perspective of Darwinian natural selection, does not cohere with the biblical portrayal of creation. Theologians such as B. B. Warfield, and even Machen himself, were not at all sure that this was the situation. The liberal establishment, however, was convinced that this was the case, and consequently jettisoned the creation narratives of Genesis as the stuff of mere myth for the more intellectually rigorous and respectable tenets of science. Bryan aimed at the surface, while Machen aimed a little lower at the foundation, at the sea change occurring regarding authority.

This paradigm shift came with many consequences. Liberalism could not entirely follow modernism, for it could not abandon faith and religion altogether. It consequently forged a middle road between secular modernism and fundamentalism. In order to maintain this middle position, it simply applied faith to certain areas of life and reason to others. What counts for knowledge in the real world—namely, scientific evidence—does not count for knowledge in the spiritual world. Faith and reason are cut asunder and compartmentalized. The upshot is that faith is largely conceived of as a personal experience. It is true, but not in the same sense that mathematical axioms, such as $2 + 2 = 4$, are true. Rather, it is true in a personal and experiential way. Thus, liberalism attempted to retain the value, even high value, of religion, while being thoroughly modern.

This approach of liberalism poses obvious problems for biblical Christianity, not the least of which is the role of historical events in demonstrating Christianity's truthfulness. Machen takes up this issue in his books *The Origin of Paul's Religion* and *The Virgin Birth of Christ*, as well as elsewhere. Another significant problem that this approach of liberalism raises is the betrayal of the biblical notion of faith. The denuding of faith by reducing it to personal experience was for Machen the foundational problem with liberalism. When the invitation came to speak to the vacationers at the Grove City Bible Conference, Machen saw his opportunity to engage this crucial question: What is faith? He had written on the subject before, contributing his solicited essay on "My Idea of God" to *The Women's Home Companion*, and he preached on it during his time in the pulpit at First Presbyterian Church. His finished product, *What Is Faith?*, was published in the fall of 1925, making Machen's thought available to wider audiences and readers yet to come. In typical fashion, Machen offers much more than mere polemics in this book. He dismantles the liberal notion of faith, to be sure, but he also explores the lush contours and rich textures of faith, the central treasure of Christianity.

Faith Versus Faith in . . .

Machen begins by pointing out that for some, the question "What is faith?" may seem unnecessary, the mere asking it to be a sign of bad manners. Essentially, he has the liberal perspective in view as he continues, "Faith, it may be said, cannot be known except by experience, and when it is known by experience, logical analysis of it, and the logical separation of it from other experiences, will only serve to destroy its power and its charm." This, Machen reveals, reflects the tendency of the day "to disparage the intellectual aspect of the religious aspect." This romantic view of faith much prefers to simply experience it than to define or analyze it, or much less prove it. By drawing attention to this perspective in these opening lines, Machen laments the derogation of faith to a lesser order than knowledge, and he prepares the reader for a view of faith diametrically opposed to the one proposed by the modernists.

Machen's charges that the liberal view smacks of anti-intellectualism may appear difficult to sustain. Liberalism emanated from some of the country's most prestigious academic institutions, including the divinity schools at Harvard, Yale, and the University of Chicago, and seminaries, such as Union Theological Seminary in New York. To better understand Machen's charge, as well as to grasp the fuller context of the book, it helps to consider the same question Machen raised in its historical context. Machen was certainly not the first to pose the question or wrestle with the relationship between faith and reason. The great thinkers of the Christian tradition devoted much time to the question. Augustine takes it up throughout his writings, and most of the medieval theologians, such as Anselm and Aquinas, were consumed by it.

Moving into the modern era, the question remained—only now, and in the ensuing centuries, the relation of faith to science and the enlightenment ideal of autonomous reason emerge as the central issue. In the eighteenth century, two significant German thinkers forever left their mark on the debate. First, the philosopher Immanuel Kant endeavored to save faith by severing it from knowledge and from any means of empirical or scientific investigation. Faith may not be proved through science, but it cannot be disproved

5.1. William Jennings Bryan's invitation for Machen to testify at the Scopes Monkey Trial, the first trial to be dubbed "The Trial of the Twentieth Century." Machen declined the offer.

either. In a sophisticated (and complicated) way, he divided faith and knowledge, putting them in quite literally two different worlds. Adding to Kant's thought, at the tail end of the eighteenth century, the theologian Friedrich Schleiermacher further alienated faith from knowledge in his classic text *On Religion, Speeches to Its Cultured Despisers* (1799). The cultured despisers were the young university students who, in their commitment to science and reason, saw no need for religion; they had progressed beyond it. Schleiermacher urged them to take another look. Considered to be the father of modern liberalism, Schleiermacher argued that religion is good or useful not because it is true in any objective or scientific sense. It is purely experiential, life-enhancing and enriching. Without it, Schleiermacher warned the cultured despisers, both individual life and culture are impoverished.

This intellectual and theological revolution took some time to reach American shores. But when it did, it announced itself with bravado. William James quickly legitimized Schleiermacher's argument by appealing to the psychological value of religion in his famous work *Varieties of Religious Experience* (1902). And liberalism gave this viewpoint a welcome home in its attempt to speak to America's own cultured despisers of religion. What Machen shows in this work, as well as elsewhere, is the irony inherent in this project. While it is intended to rescue Christianity by recasting faith, it actually destroys Christianity precisely through that recasting. In fact, for him, this may very well encapsulate the crux of the problem.

Against the "passionate anti-intellectualism" of liberalism, which Machen also refers to in this book as "naturalism" or the "Modern Church," he asserts, "As a matter of fact, all true faith involves an intellectual element; all faith involves knowledge and issues in knowledge." Machen can't, in other words, view faith apart from what that faith is in, which is to say he can't view faith apart from the content of faith. This becomes the thesis of his book, and after a lengthy introduction, he devotes seven chapters to fully exhibiting the content of faith: the knowledge that it consists of and the life that issues from it. As he argued in *Christianity and Liberalism,* anything less is not a version of Christian faith; it is something different altogether.

But, also as in *Christianity and Liberalism,* Machen realizes that this book flies in the face of contemporary sensibilities. Consequently, he and his writings will once again meet, perhaps even spark, controversy. Machen does not wince, however. To him, it is too important a question to not raise and to answer rightly. The question "What is faith?" is of the utmost practical and theoretical importance to the church; it cannot be brushed aside. Besides, in these last years Machen has learned some things about controversy and its value. He observes, "Controversy of the right sort is good; for out of such controversy, as church history and Scripture alike teach, there comes the salvation of souls." One of the reviewers in *The British Weekly* agreed, observing, "It is a book of controversy in the highest and most honourable sense of the word."

The previous school year at Princeton Theological Seminary offered Machen evidence of the value of this type of controversy. A certain indifference among the student body regarding theology and the central things of Christianity led to a superficial religious life. That all dissipated through the controversy—which, from our vantage point, we can see as only beginning at Princeton at that time—that forced the students out of their lethargy and on to rigorous thought. Machen even likens it to an awakening, describing the impact this way: "Youth has begun to think for itself; the evil of compromising associations has been discovered; Christian heroism in the face of opposition has come again to its rights; a new interest has been aroused in the historical and philosophical questions that underlie the Christian religion; true and independent convictions have been formed." Once again, Machen does not dodge the challenge. The question is simply too crucial, the consequences are of too high a value, for Machen not to ask, "What is faith?"

Away with All Pale Abstractions

While Harry Emerson Fosdick served as one of the targets in *Christianity and Liberalism*, here the work of Arthur Cushman McGiffert, among others, receives attention. McGiffert, educated at Union Seminary and taking a Ph.D. from Marburg, Germany, was one of the leading exponents of German liberalism in America. He studied under and maintained a close relationship with leading liberal German theologian Adolf Harnack. Earlier, in 1897, McGiffert, a Presbyterian, had found himself facing heresy charges because of his book *A History of Christianity in the Apostolic Age*. He voluntarily moved his credentials to Congregationalism to avoid a trial, but he retained his post as professor of church history at Union, even serving as Union's president in the crucial years 1917 to 1926. Well familiar with McGiffert, Machen focuses on his most recent work at the time, *The God of the Early Christians* (1924).

In this book, McGiffert argues for a new way of thinking about theism that would require abandoning a conception of a personal God in favor of an abstract concept of goodness, allowing us moderns, Machen observes of McGiffert's view, to "be religious men." In the end, McGiffert proposes an "antitheistic or non-theistic religion" that looks to God as more of an idea than a person. Machen notes, "The interesting thing about this remarkable theory is not found in any likelihood of its truth; for it is not really difficult to refute; but is found in the connection between the theory and the anti-intellectualist trend of the modern world." Instead of McGiffert's take, Machen notes that the Christian's response is clear: "Away with all pale abstractions." It is not an idea of goodness, but God, the creator, the ruler of the universe, the redeemer, who gives Christianity its basis.

Machen ends this chapter by discussing how God might be known. He observes that God may be known in cosmos. Quoting the psalmist, Machen affirms, " 'The heavens declare the glory of God; and the firmament showeth his handiwork' " (Ps. 19:1). To some, however, this glory goes unperceived because of the blinding effects of sin. God is also known through the conscience. Supremely, however, God is known through the Bible. To be sure, Machen acknowledges that the Bible reinforces the knowledge of God in natural revelation, "but it does far more than all that; it also presents God in loving action, in the course of history, for the salvation of sinful men." This is the grand story that reveals the depth of God and the rich contours of his relationship to humanity. As Machen declares, "In the Bible we see God in action; we see Him in fiery indignation wiping out the foulness of Sodom; we see Him leading Israel like a flock; we see Him giving His only begotten Son for the sins of the world. And by what we see we learn to know Him." And this is what Machen concludes that we learn: "In all His varied dealings with His people He has never failed; so now we know Him and adore Him." We learn that God is sufficient for our needs and that he is our champion. God who is in every way for us so that nothing can be against us is not an abstraction, but the living, true God.

The Christian also cries, "Away with all pale abstractions" when it comes to Christ. It is necessary, Machen points out, when speaking of the Christian God to speak of

Christ. And it is necessary further still to speak of Christ not in mere abstractions, but as he is presented in Scripture. Consequently, in chapter 3 of his book, Machen offers a sustained criticism of a religion that makes Jesus the mere example of faith, and not the object of faith. His example is useful, but, Machen argues, only after redemption, not before. As Machen says, "There is a child's hymn that puts the matter right:

> O dearly, dearly has He loved,
> And we must love Him too,
> And trust in His redeeming blood,
> And try His works to do."

He adds, "This is the true order of Christian pedagogy— 'trust in His redeeming blood' first, and then 'try his works to do.' Disaster always follows when that order is reversed."

This leads Machen to present once again his well-worn position of the absolute necessity of the orthodox view of Christ as the God-man, "the battle ground of theologians." In a memorable line, he quips, "The next thing less than the infinite is infinitely less." No matter how high one's view of Christ may be, Machen points out, if he is not viewed as God then he is no Savior, no forgiver of sins. But Machen moves beyond polemics to offer readers a glimpse of the great consolation and comfort that the crucial doctrine of the deity of Christ brings. Readily admitting that there is mystery in the union of the human and divine natures of the person of Christ and mystery in the union of the members of the Trinity, Machen exclaims that it is a mystery that we can rejoice in. He explains, "[Christ] is on the throne; He is at the centre; He is ground and explanation of all things; He pervades the remotest bounds; by Him all things consist. The world is full of dread, mysterious powers; they touch us already in a thousand woes. But from all of them we are safe." We are safe because of Christ. Not a Christ who is a mere fellow-sufferer who happened upon a unique relationship with God, but Christ who is at once both the God of the universe and the bearer of our infirmities.

Our Deadly Need

There is a necessary corollary to Machen's high view of Christ and his work. It is one that Machen viewed his contemporaries as being loath to accept: a low view of humanity, unable to overcome the sinful condition. As Machen begins his fourth chapter, "Faith Born of Need," he makes this connection, noting, "It is not enough for us to know that Jesus is great and good. . . . If we are to trust Jesus, we must come to him personally and individually with some need of the soul that he alone can relieve." And he continues, "That need of the soul from which Jesus alone can save is sin." Machen, as he did in teaching about God and Christ, wants to avoid abstractions on this point. It's not merely the concept of sin, or "the sins of the world or the sins of other people, but I mean your sin—your sin and mine." Shedding politeness, Machen uses the first person and the second-person singular to put an exclamation point on our need.

All of this talk leads Machen to nostalgic reflection on "the old way of coming to Christ, first penitence at the dread voice of the law, then joy at the gracious invitation of the Saviour." That way has succumbed to the new: "Nothing is more characteristic of present religious conditions than the loss of the consciousness of sin; confidence in human resources has now been substituted for the thankful acceptance of the grace of God." Though this "optimism of human worth" was not quite as strong as it had been at the turn of the twentieth century prior to World War I, it nevertheless abounded in liberalism, which parted ways with the biblical portrayal of humanity and sin. This new perspective also infiltrated education. As testimony to Machen's abilities to see the broad implications and complexities of the theological shifts in liberalism, he turns his attention to the "Morality Code" of the Character Education Institute in Washington, D.C., with such commands as "Good Americans play fair" and "Good Americans are self-reliant." Machen castigates this approach for grounding morality in nothing more than patriotism and pragmatism.

Against the flow of both modern theology and modern culture, Machen advocates a return to the biblical portrayal of humanity as lost and in desperate need of salvation, leading him further into doctrine. Consequently, in chapters 5 and 6, he addresses the bedrock doctrines of Christ's atonement on the cross and justification by faith. Again, Machen acknowledges that in so doing he might very well be quite out of step. He predicts that objections to his choice of words will likely follow, noting, " 'Justification,' it will be said, is a distressingly long word; and as for the word 'doctrine,' that has a forbidding sound." He adds, "Many persons are horrified by the use of a theological term; they seem to have a notion that modern Christians must be addressed always in words of one syllable." Machen wants to resist this tendency with all his might. Not because he is curmudgeonly, but because substitutes simply won't do. Precise terminology accurately unpacks the biblical teaching, and in this case, accuracy is everything. It is a matter of life and death.

Justification by faith is consequently crucial because it gets to the heart of saving faith. Machen puts the matter this way: "The efficacy of faith, then, depends not on the faith itself, considered as a psychological phenomenon, but upon the object of the faith, namely Christ." We are redeemed,

Machen continues, not on account of faith, but through or by means of faith, as "faith is merely the means which the Holy Spirit uses to apply to the individual soul the benefits of Christ's death." This view points beyond the individual as meriting God's favor in any way. Instead, it looks to the cross and the all-sufficient Savior as accomplishing salvation. And this, Machen says, is the doctrine of justification by faith, "a liberating doctrine in the history of the world."

The Life of Faith

The final question that Machen takes up in *What Is Faith?* concerns the life of faith, which he gets at through two chapters on faith's relationship to works and hope, respectively. Relating faith and works has always been challenging for the church; the problem stumped even Martin Luther. Machen explains how it has become such a challenge by pointing to the passive nature of faith and salvation, while at the same time acknowledging the abounding ethical commands expected of the child of God. Machen reiterates that the doctrine of justification by faith demands that salvation "depends altogether on God. . . . Acceptance with God is not something that we earn; it is not something that is subject to the wretched uncertainties of human endeavor." This, Machen notes, "is really presupposed in the whole New Testament; but it is made particularly plain in the Epistles of Paul." Machen adds, however, "In the Epistle of James there seems at first sight to be a discordant note in this great New Testament chorus"—his emphasis is on *seems*.

He reconciles the difficulty first by pointing out what James is not doing: "[James] is no advocate of a mere 'gospel street-cleaning'; he is no advocate of what is falsely called to-day a 'practical,' as distinguished from a doctrinal, Christianity; he is not a man who seeks to drown out an inward disquiet by a bustling philanthropy." The point that James is making, with which Paul concurs, is that "men who had been saved by faith could not continue to live unholy lives." Playing off the New Testament analogy of the new birth, Machen points out that in birth one is passive, not contributing at all. He then adds, "But birth is followed by life: and though a man is not active in his birth he is active in the life that follows." The new birth, Machen notes in applying the analogy, is followed by the new life, a life of active obedience. Even here, however, God's power is at work within the individual, enabling and accomplishing good works. So he concludes the chapter by quoting Zechariah 4:6: "Not by might, nor by power, but by my Spirit, says the LORD of hosts."

This leaves one final question for Machen to address: the relationship of faith and hope, which he casts as the goal of the life of faith. The hope that Machen has in mind resides in another place, the hope of heaven and eternal reward. In raising this issue, Machen cannot help but to address one further problem with liberalism. Machen points out that Christ's teaching on heaven and the hope of eternal rewards makes no sense without the counterpart teaching on hell and the judgment seat, the latter elements being jettisoned by liberalism. In many places Jesus contrasts eternal blessedness with eternal woe, heaven with hell. This leads Machen to conclude, "If this element were removed, what would be left? Certainly not the gospel itself, certainly not the good news of Jesus' saving work; for that is concerned with these high issues of eternal life and death." There are two sides to the good news.

Yet Machen again moves beyond polemics in this final chapter. He ends by discussing that while our hope of heaven is sure and our faith is certain, our realization of that hope and our exercise of faith sometimes wane. So he offers his parting advice:

> Even very imperfect and very weak faith is sufficient for salvation; salvation does not depend upon the strength of our faith, but it depends on Christ. When you want assurance of salvation, think not about your faith, but about the Person who is the object of your faith. . . . He will not desert those who are committed to Him, but will keep them safe both in this world and in that which is to come.

Conclusion

The year after Machen wrote *What Is Faith?*, he was elected by the seminary directors to the chair of apologetics at Princeton. As explained further in other chapters, because of political machinations the appointment never materialized. Nevertheless, the proposal to move him from New Testament to apologetics reflects Machen's capabilities in the task of defending and persuasively proclaiming the faith. And *What Is Faith?* is Exhibit A. Here he cogently responds to liberal attempts to denude God and Christ, the gospel and salvation, and faith and hope of meaning, vitality, and transformative power. Additionally, he wrestles with the perennial challenge in apologetics: articulating the relationship of faith and reason. He makes a strong case for a robust view of faith. Yet in the process, he does not adopt a naive view of reason. Following his mentor, B. B. Warfield, Machen advocates "right reason," a term coined by the elder Princetonian. What Warfield and Machen intended by this construct was to highlight the ethical dimension to knowledge. A regenerated person reasons rightly; an unregenerated person does not.

A number of interpreters tend to see the emphasis on reason in both Warfield and Machen as more reflective of following the philosophy of Scottish common sense realism
than their biblical and theological commitments. Common
sense philosophy, developed by Thomas Reid and brought
to America by the two Scottish presidents of Princeton, John
Witherspoon and James McCosh, emphasized reason and
the responsible use of the senses in arriving at an objective
understanding of the world. This was far from the views of
idealist philosophers such as John Locke and Immanuel
Kant and theologians, such as Schleiermacher and Harnack
in Germany and Fosdick and McGiffert in America, who followed the idealist tradition. While it is true that both Warfield
and Machen held that there is such a thing as an objective
knowledge of the world, they did so in such a way as to distance themselves from some main tenets of common sense
realism. Consequently, Machen affirms not only that Christianity is true for those who accept it, but that "it is true," in
an objective, absolute sense. Yet here is the crucial factor, as
Machen notes: "But for a thing to be true is one thing and
for it to be recognized as true is another." He continues, "In
order that Christianity may be recognized as true by men
upon this earth the blinding effects of sin must be removed."
And this is done, he argues, only by the work of regenera-
tion by the Holy Spirit. This work, however, "does not stand
in opposition to a truly scientific attitude towards the evidence, but on the contrary it is necessary in order that the
truly scientific attitude may be attained; it is not a substitute
for the intellect, but on the contrary by it the intellect is made
to be a trustworthy instrument for apprehending truth."

Machen sees it this way: the natural mind is bent away
from seeing the truth. In fact, it distorts the truth. The work
of the Holy Spirit enables one to grasp the truth. And this
he saw as the problem with liberalism as it engaged the

modern world. Rather than confront the modernist view that reasoning and science leave no room for God, liberalism instead simply turned to faith, a faith that was merely experiential, sentimental, and personal. Machen called for a different response to the challenge of modernity, one that would not run from the intellectual challenge, but that would meet it. And, of course, he knew that the battle for truth was ultimately a spiritual one. Perhaps the *Westminster Shorter Catechism*, which Machen quotes on this precise point, captures the matter best: "What is effectual calling? Effectual calling is the work of God's Spirit, whereby, convincing us of our sin and misery, enlightening our minds in the knowledge of Christ, and renewing our wills, He doth persuade and enable us to embrace Jesus Christ, freely offered to us in the gospel."

A Note on the Sources

What Is Faith?, first published in 1925 by Macmillan, has been reprinted by The Banner of Truth Trust (1991). Machen reviewed McGiffert's *The God of the Early Christians* in the *Princeton Theological Review*, vol. 22 (1924), 544–88. For a thorough, scholarly treatment of McGiffert in particular and the development of liberalism in general, see Gary Dorrien's *The Making of American Liberal Theology: Imagining Progressive Religion, 1805–1900* (2001) and *The Making of American Liberal Theology: Idealism, Realism, and Modernity, 1900–1950* (2003). For a treatment of Scottish realism and the Princetonians, see George Marsden, *Understanding Fundamentalism and Evangelicalism* (1991), 122–52. For brief discussions of *What Is Faith?*, see Ned B. Stonehouse, *J. Gresham Machen* (1986), 394–400; D. G. Hart, *Defending the Faith* (1994), 91–103; and Terry A. Chrisope, *Toward a Sure Faith* (2000), 177–83.

6

A LEGACY OF SCHOLARSHIP:
THE ORIGIN OF PAUL'S RELIGION
AND THE VIRGIN BIRTH
OF CHRIST

For I would have you know, brothers,
the gospel that was preached by me
is not man's gospel.
For I did not receive it from any man,
nor was I taught it,
but I received it through a revelation of Jesus Christ.

Galatians 1:11–12

Your book [The Virgin Birth] *is not one to read when*
groggy with sleep.

Mary Gresham Machen to J. Gresham Machen

A significant aspect of J. Gresham Machen's legacy concerns his contribution as a New Testament scholar. His work has been hailed as a benchmark for twentieth-century conservative scholarship. Quite recently, a president of the Evangelical Theological Society singled out Machen's work as a model for the type of scholarship that young theologians and biblical scholars should endeavor to emulate, extending Machen's standard-setting work into the twenty-first century. This piece of his legacy owes to his two books spanning the busy decade of the 1920s, *The Origin of Paul's Religion,* published in 1921, and *The Virgin Birth of Christ,* published in 1930.

As Painful as Pulling Teeth

Depending on how you measure it, either *The Origin of Paul's Religion* was a decade in the making, or it was a product of merely months. Regardless, it did not come easily to Machen, as he wrote, "The last two mornings have been devoted without interruption to writing on my book. It has been painful as pulling teeth. I suffered intensely; I paced the floor in agony; I dawdled because nothing would come to me." That letter was written in the summer of 1920. Machen was busy spending his summer vacation preparing to deliver the James Sprunt lectures at Union Theological Seminary in Richmond, Virginia, the next January. Union had wanted Machen to join the faculty back in 1915. He declined, attributing the reason to his being "deeply rooted" at Princeton. The president of the seminary, W. W. Moore, at least pulled a consolation prize out of the negotiations, getting Machen to commit to deliver the 1921 Sprunt lectures. When he agreed in 1915, he thought he had all the time in the world, and from the beginning planned to use the lectures as the material from which he could publish his first major book.

But then the war occurred, and Machen, serving from January 1918 to March 1919, pushed aside the research and preparation. Then in 1920 he found himself embroiled in the first wave of the controversy in the Presbyterian Church in the U.S.A., when the plan of union was discussed at the General Assembly. So, with the years evaporating, Machen found himself struggling to work on his book in July and August, knowing that he would have a full load of teaching that fall semester at Princeton. He was also preaching quite a bit that summer and on into the fall. It was at those engagements, however, that he found the best time to write. He would typically either arrive early or stay late, using Saturday or Monday in his hotel room to write. He found the Hotel Dupont particularly amenable. As Machen wrote, "There is something about the eleventh floor of the Hotel Dupont that stimulates literary activity." He apparently wrote best in the mornings. And fortunately, in addition to those uninterrupted times in hotels when he could write, his classes that fall at Princeton did not begin until 10:30. He completed the lectures, putting the finishing touches on them over Christmas, and boarded the train for Richmond.

The lectures went off brilliantly. Machen threw himself into the work and into the life of the seminary during his short stay there. The remuneration was also quite agreeable. At $1,400, it was over half his salary that year from Princeton Seminary, and in today's economy it would be a significant amount. That spring he revised the manuscript one last time before sending it off to Macmillan. He received a contract, although it required him to cut quite a few pages from the bulky manuscript, and the book appeared in October 1921.

But it is not quite accurate to see him beginning the book in the summer of 1920. He had published an article containing the germ of the book's thesis in 1912, and he had taught on the subject all through the 1910s. The book, consequently, reflects both years of rigorous research and thought and also a freshness and vitality of those writing episodes on the eleventh floor of the Hotel Dupont and mornings at Princeton. In fact, much the same can be said of *The Virgin Birth of Christ*. With it, however, the years of preparation were even longer and the intensity of the actual writing even greater. The thesis and ideas of that book first began to take shape in Machen's mind when he was a student at Princeton. In 1905 and 1906, Machen's two-part article on "The New Testament Account on the Birth of Jesus" appeared in the *Princeton Theological Review*. This was Machen's student paper during his senior year at Princeton Seminary, for which he won the Maitland Prize, securing the publishing of his article and providing him with a year's fellowship for study in Germany. It also essentially paved the way for his appointment to the faculty at Princeton. He regularly taught courses on the birth narratives in the gospels throughout his teaching at Princeton.

He did not assemble all of these thoughts, however, until the 1929–30 school year. That, it may be recalled, was perhaps one of the busiest times of his life. Having been routed out of Princeton, he was in the throes of establishing Westminster Seminary in Philadelphia. Again, he found the mornings his best time to write. And given that he was the principal agent in founding the seminary, he could very easily arrange his classes to fit his writing schedule. It was, however, no less tortuous for him not only to find the time, but also to actually do the writing.

The end products in both cases, however, well repay his effort. Both books were considered by friend and foe alike to be models of scholarship, brilliantly executed, and significant contributions to the field. They also provided theological conservatives with plenty of ammunition in the battle with liberalism. Here was not a mere trifle of a response to liberalism, or simply a dismissal of liberalism by an appeal to a "Thus says the Lord" style of apologetics. In both books, he met the liberal scholar on his own ground, provided thorough arguments, and, in the words of one reviewer of *The Origin of Paul's Religion*, made "all Christians his debtors." The book was largely the reason that Hampden-Sydney College awarded Machen an honorary Doctor of Divinity degree in 1922. *The Virgin Birth* met with no less critical acclaim.

In the pages that follow we will explore these two works by Machen, beginning first with *The Origin of Paul's Religion* and proceeding to *The Virgin Birth of Christ*. First, however, a brief detour looks at the rise and development of higher criticism of the Bible in order to gain the fuller context of Machen's contribution in these two books.

The Bible and Higher Criticism

In the early nineteenth century, certain scholars in the field of Old Testament studies began to question the Mosaic authorship of the Pentateuch, offering instead the view that the first five books of the Bible may be traced to four different authorial strands deriving from a much later date than that of Moses. The end product was thought to have then been collated by an editor, perhaps Hezekiah or someone quite like him. This approach forever marked a new direction in biblical scholarship. A radical criticism evolved that took as a starting point the position that the Bible is not a divinely inspired book, but a human one, deriving from a religious community and traced with legend and myth.

Before too long, a group of scholars under the leadership of Ferdinand Christian Bauer at the University of Tübingen in Germany applied this methodology to the gospels. This group of scholars and their approach to the New Testament became known as the "Tübingen School." One of the more famous of the products of this school is David Friedrich Strauss's two-volume *Life of Jesus, Critically Examined* in 1835–36. Strauss proposed that there was the historical Jesus and then there was the Jesus of myth, the Jesus created by the overzealous community of his followers and the Jesus who appears in the gospels. From this view developed a cottage industry of books pursuing the "quest for the historical Jesus." The approach to the Pentateuch and the gospels tumbled on to the Pauline epistles. There, too, it was argued that Paul was not the actual author of these thirteen books, but that they derived from the Christian community with his name attached as a means of gaining credibility or of simply identifying with his thought.

A basic antisupernaturalistic presupposition underlies this approach. That is to say, there is a foundational commitment to the belief that the Bible is simply a natural book written by fallible human beings who couched their sense of history and their understanding of their religious leaders in terms of myth and legend and miracle. This school of thought, however, was not ready to dismiss religion altogether. Consequently, it sought to look beyond the myth to find the element of truth that embodied a deeper, even spiritual, sense of life and the world. In the process, this view severed religion from being rooted in historical events and in the factuality of the biblical text. The virgin birth thus becomes a powerful symbol of Christ's uniqueness, but not a historical fact; the cross and the resurrection embody the hopes and aspirations of the church and represent both the human condition and salvation, but they were not real events occurring in space and time.

Machen was well schooled in the teachings and methodology of this approach, learning of it firsthand while studying in Germany. Yet he found it to be quite deficient, and far from being a progenitor of a more robust religion for the modern era, he viewed it as the destruction of any meaningful religion whatsoever. In these books he takes up two of the significant challenges made by the Tübingen School and other manifestations of higher criticism. The first concerns the origin of Paul's religion, which very much turns on the historical events of the cross and the resurrection. In the second, he explores the gospel accounts of the virgin birth. Curiously, he does so by using higher criticism's methodology against itself. This is seen first in his argument in *The Origin of Paul's Religion*.

The Riddle of Paul

The question of the origin of Paul's religion may strike some as rather obvious and, perhaps, others as rather insignificant. Yet to Machen, there could not be a more crucial question, neither could there be one more worth pursuing, even if the pursuit meant a 300-plus-page book (which would have been closer to 500 pages if Machen had won over his publisher). Machen put the reason this way: "Explain the origin of the religion of Paul and you have solved the problem of the origin of Christianity." At bottom, the question derived entirely from the effects of higher criticism on the understanding of the Bible. Since the Bible is not a supernatural book, then Christianity, it argued, is not a privileged religion. Instead, it is on par with all other religions and its origin can be explained in merely sociological terms.

Three such options were offered from the liberal perspective. First, there is the old-line liberal view, represented by Albrecht Ritschl and Adolf von Harnack. This view has Paul "deifying" Christ. It argues, as Machen summarizes, that the disciples, after the death of Christ, attributed to Christ "a kind of religious importance which He had never claimed," even beginning to "ascribe to him divine attributes." Yet this process could go only so far with the disciples, since they knew Jesus personally; however, as Machen

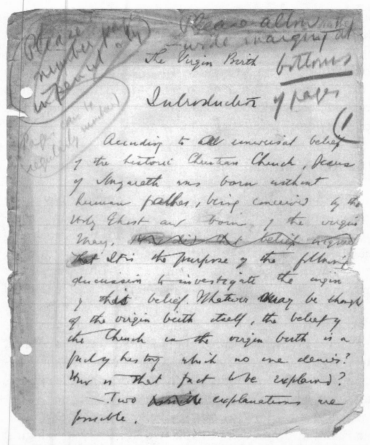

6.1. Machen's handwritten manuscript of *The Virgin Birth of Christ*, with his own editing and instructions to the typist.

continues his summary, "In the case of the apostle Paul, who had never seen him, the process of deification could go unchecked." In short, old-line liberalism held that Paul himself, with his fanciful imagination and his hallucinations such as the experience on the Damascus road, is the origin of Paul's religion.

That was the story up until about 1900. Then two challenges to this view, still within liberalism, emerged. The first, held by Wilhelm Wrede and annunciated in his 1904 book *Paulus,* argues that Paul proffered a distinct religion from the teachings and life of Jesus of Nazareth. Paul founded his religion on certain Jewish conceptions of the Messiah, derived from the Old Testament and intertestamental literature, but not on Jesus. The third trajectory comes from Wilhelm Bousset and his 1913 *Kyrios Christos.* Bousset agreed with Wrede that Paul did not derive his religion from Christ. But, with a stroke of originality, he looked to pagan religions, especially the mystery religions of the Greco-Roman world, as the source. Of the three views, Bousset's held sway at the time Machen wrote *The Origin of Paul's Religion.*

Machen outlines these three views in the first chapter, which is the introduction. He proceeds first to examine these views in light of the historical evidence and second to pit them against each other. Consequently, he both positively and negatively shows them to be false and the alternative to be true. The alternative is simply to say that the origin of Paul's religion is Jesus, not the Jesus of Paul's or of the disciples' imagination, but the Jesus of history, the supernatural God-man of the gospel accounts. Paul met Jesus in a unique way along the Damascus road, and as he testifies later in Galatians 1:11–12, this encounter served as Paul's gateway to the gospel and the basis for his apostleship. This thesis, that the origin of Paul's religion is in full concert with the person and work of Christ, comes out most forcefully in chapter 4, entitled "Paul and Jesus," perhaps the prime chapter of the book. That chapter is preceded by two chapters tracing Paul's life. The first follows Paul from his early years and devout Judaism, ending with his conversion. The next one, chapter 3, covers the time from his conversion through his ascendancy and his work as an apostle. Chapter 5 engages the work of Wrede, with chapters 6, 7, and 8 given over to the more prominent thought of Bousset.

In these latter chapters, Machen pits Wrede's research and conclusions against Bousset's, using them to cancel each other out. He also shows that the respective views do not withstand scrutiny. First, concerning Wrede, who argued that Paul derived his gospel from pre-Christian Judaism and not from Jesus, Machen notes that Paul was not in concert with first-century Judaism on the two counts of the law and human sinfulness and of the Messiah. The Pharisees, while typically thought of as being zealous for the law, in reality minimized the law by getting around it. In the process, they denied the utter sinfulness of the heart and humanity's inability to overcome sin. As Machen notes, "It is easier to clean the outside of the cup than it is to cleanse the heart." The Pharisees were experts at cleaning the cup, and Paul, before his conversion, was not to be outdone in the activity. Consequently, the deep sense of sin that permeates Paul's writings did not derive from first-century Judaism. Neither, Machen argues, did his understanding of Christ as the Messiah.

When Machen turns to Bousset in the last three chapters, he points out that Bousset sees the Pauline conceptions of the new birth or the new creation, the sacraments, and Christ's work of redemption as all sourced in pagan or Hellenistic religions. Machen shows that any parallels are entirely on the surface, if at all, and that Paul's actual teachings on these issues are far and away different from any pagan source. Both Wrede and Bousset advance intriguing theories; they simply, however, lack evidence. This leads Machen to the conclusion that if the alternatives fail to account for the data, then perhaps what Paul says about the origin of his religion should be given its due. And this Machen develops most thoroughly in chapter 4.

There are many parallels between chapter 4 of *The Origin of Paul's Religion* and *Christianity and Liberalism*. In fact, some paragraphs look uncannily similar. Machen observes, "[Paul] regarded Christ as Lord and Master, and he identified that Christ fully with the Jesus who had lived but a few years before. This testimony must be faced and invalidated by those who would find the origin of Paul's religion elsewhere than in Jesus of Nazareth." One thing Machen cleverly points out is that Paul never defended his view of Christ as the God-man, noting, "The tremendous doctrine of the person of Christ is never defended, but always assumed." This takes on significance given Paul's clash with the Judaizers. While they challenged Paul's teaching on his view of Gentile freedom, they never raised an objection to his teaching on the person of Christ, which Machen takes as reflecting that the early apostles, besides Paul, held to the deity of Christ, and that the deity of Christ is clearly taught in the gospels. Consequently, both Paul and the gospel writers agree, Jesus is both supernatural and the redeemer. And that, Machen demonstrates, is the heart of Paul's religion and the essence of Christianity.

This leads Machen to develop a key thesis of the book, that the religion of Paul, and hence Christianity, "is a religion of redemption." He brings this out forcefully in the last paragraph of the book:

> [Christ] "loved me and gave Himself for me." There lies the basis of the religion of Paul; there lies the basis of all of Christianity. . . . The religion of Paul was not founded upon a complex of ideas derived from Judaism or from paganism. It was founded upon the historical Jesus. But the historical Jesus upon whom it was founded was not the Jesus of modern reconstruction, but the Jesus of the whole New Testament and of the Christian faith; not a teacher who survived in the memory of His disciples, but the Saviour who after His redeeming work was done still lived and could still be loved.

Watching Machen navigate the labyrinthine contours of the Pauline scholarship of his day reminds one of the oft-quoted saying that has been attributed to any number of people: "We may not exactly follow everything he says, but we're certainly glad that he's on our side." This reminds us well of Paul's body metaphor of the church. While not everyone is called to be a scholar, some are, and some, like Machen, use those gifts and abilities to edify the whole body—even if not all members of the body are aware or appreciative of the efforts. He equally applied those talents to another crucial question lurking among the modernist controversy—the virgin birth of Christ.

Not Bedtime Reading

Fosdick's sermon "Shall the Fundamentalists Win?," already discussed in relationship to Machen's *Christianity and Liberalism,* also sheds some light on what Machen was doing in *The Virgin Birth of Christ.* Fosdick sketched two views. The first, the orthodox view, is "that the virgin birth is to be accepted as historical fact." The second sees the virgin birth as mythical language to point to Christ's uniqueness. To be sure, "they phrased it in terms of a biological miracle," but, he adds, that is such a construct "that our modern minds cannot use." He then asks, "Is not the Christian church large enough to hold within her hospitable fellowship people who differ on points like this and agree to differ until further truth be manifested?" Machen offered a resounding "no," both in *Christianity and Liberalism* and in *The Virgin Birth of Christ,* only in the latter, his "no" lasted just under 400 pages.

His own mother had this to say: "Your book is not one to read when groggy with sleep." And Machen himself, reflecting on the book with a good dash of self-deprecating humor, offered, "Whether it is a good book is a question I shall not presume to answer, but no one can deny that it is a big one." It is his magnum opus, representative of decades of thought and numerous lectures and many articles. It remains unrivaled in its contribution to the New Testament scholarship on these important narratives in the gospels. Certainly, scholarship has advanced since Machen wrote, leaving some of the book obsolete. Yet one is hard-pressed to consider any replacement of Machen's book that deals as thoroughly and as competently with the biblical material on the virgin birth.

As mentioned earlier, the book came at a busy time for Machen. It was published during the first year of Westminster Seminary's existence. Those engaged in academic work know that even in ordinary times the academic year can be exhausting. Given that it was the first year of Westminster and that Machen was the chief force behind the school, and that his ongoing struggles within the Presbyterian Church in the U.S.A. were nagging him, the academic year of 1929–30 drained the life out of him. Yet, remarkably, he found time to finish the book and see it through to publication. Of course, he was helped by his decades of investment in the subject and publication of earlier writings, mostly in the *Princeton Theological Review*. And Machen was no stranger to the controversies that the book addresses.

As with the question of the origin of Paul's religion, the virgin birth became an issue because of the onset of higher criticism. For centuries, this cherished and central belief of the church, except for the case of heretical groups, went largely unchallenged. The biblical narratives were taken at face value, and the miracle of the virgin birth caused no discontent. But as Fosdick points out, the virgin birth runs counter to modern sensibilities; such things simply do not occur. This leaves the reader of the Bible with two options: either accept the biblical account as true and therefore be out of step with modernism, or view it as in error. If it is in error, then one has to account for its prominence both in the biblical text and in Christianity. This leaves the critical scholar with two options, the same two options that presented themselves in the case of the origin of Paul's religion. Either the source of the error is Judaism or it is in paganism or the Hellenistic religions. Machen spends the bulk of the book, the first eleven chapters, walking through the evidence supporting the view that the virgin birth is true. He looks at the belief in the second century of the church in the first chapter and then offers a thorough investigation of the birth narratives in Luke and Matthew. He also relates these narratives to secular history and to other portions of the New Testament. Having established the warrant for the historicity of the virgin birth, he turns his attention to the opposing views in the next three chapters, offering a final chapter to reiterate his conclusions and draw out the crucial implications. He concisely summarizes his lengthy and complex arguments in this final chapter, which offers the reader a helpful guide to the book.

In his summary, he first points out that the virgin birth was not simply appended to the gospels, and that it was not a late addition written into the gospel accounts by overzealous disciples wishing to make more of Christ than he ever claimed for himself. Instead, Machen shows that the account of the virgin birth had "original place in the First and Third Gospels and was plainly attested in Palestinian sources, oral or written, underlying those Gospels." He also demonstrates that while Matthew and Luke are independent voices in giving the account, they do not contradict each other; the rest of the New Testament does not contradict them, either. His exposition of the early chapters of Matthew and Luke reflects anything but a naive view of the gospels' composition. In fact, rigidly conservative readers might flinch at all his talk concerning sources underlying the text. But Machen does not in any way intend to detract from the supernatural origin of the gospels or from their status as inspired texts. His way of handling the situation, however, shows that he knew quite well the terrain of New Testament scholarship, that he navigated it skillfully, and that he made both informed and compelling arguments.

Machen also shows how the alternative theories, that the virgin birth is an error, break down. He first points to the lack of a clear parallel or source for such a notion in Judaism. Then he shows that while certain pagan myths contain stories of supernatural births resulting from the copulation of the gods with mortals, these so-called parallels break down. Further, even if there were such a parallel, it would be impossible to see any explicit connection between these pagan accounts and the gospels. And as he did in *The Origin of Paul's Religion,* he also pits these two views, and the work of various scholars who hold them, against each other to cast aspersions on their legitimacy. He then makes the following observation: "The conclusion to which we are obliged to come after examination of the whole subject of 'alternative theories' is that if the doctrine of the virgin birth of Christ did not originate in fact, modern critical investigation has at any rate not yet succeeded in showing how it did originate." In the end, these views break down while the biblical account is consistent with itself and with historical considerations and developments.

Machen, however, is also concerned with the consequences of the view that the virgin birth is a fact. The consequences are crucial because the virgin birth is just one piece among many that form "the whole glorious picture" of who Christ presents himself to be in the pages of the

New Testament. And coming to grips with the question of who Christ is, according to Machen, constitutes "the question of all questions." The virgin birth just begins to confront the reader of the gospels with the supernatural origin and nature of Christ. It only begins to herald the message that "in the first century of our era there walked upon this earth One who was like none other among the children of men." It reminds us that at the center of Christianity is Christ, who was virgin-born in history, who lived in history, and who died and rose again in history. Without these points, one is left, in the words of B. B. Warfield as cited by Machen, with a "Christless Christianity." To reject the biblical account of the virgin birth is to view Christ as less than what he presents himself to be. As Machen put it so well in *What Is Faith?*, "The next thing less than the infinite is infinitely less." Consequently, when Fosdick suggests that the church has room both for those who accept the virgin birth as fact and for those who see it as something else, Machen insists on parting company with him. There is not room in the church, Machen argues persuasively, for those not willing to see Christ in the fullness of who he presents himself to be. There is no room for those not willing to accept the one Jesus presented in the Word of God.

Conclusion

For those accustomed to *Christianity and Liberalism*, reading *The Origin of Paul's Religion* and *The Virgin Birth of Christ* can be a bit of a stretch. These two books were written in a different style, for a different audience, and for a different purpose. Nevertheless, they are still engaging and enlightening for readers willing to invest the effort. Further, while they are certainly not as widely read or as well known as *Christianity and Liberalism*, they enshrine a significant piece of Machen's legacy. One of the most intriguing questions of Machen's life concerns his relationship to fundamentalism. Machen himself expressed that relationship ambivalently. If the choice was between liberalism or modernism on the one hand and fundamentalism on the other, then, hands down, Machen was a fundamentalist. But if he could nuance the choice, he would. A number of separate areas mark Machen off from the other fundamentalists. He was different in his politics and view of culture and in his view of the church and ministerial preparation. He was also different in his scholarship, both in nature and in kind.

Very little of the fundamentalists' literature was taken seriously by critics. Machen's work, however, got reviewed by Harnack and by Rudolf Bultmann and in the leading theological journals of all persuasions, reflecting that his contributions were a cut above. While his reviewers did not always offer ringing endorsements of his views, to a person they lauded his scholarship and acknowledged the force of his arguments. He refused merely to "preach to the choir," offering arguments that would, even if rejected, at least gain a hearing from the other side. He also strenuously avoided arguing for Christianity by his personal experience or on pietistic grounds. Machen is often likened to Bunyan's character Valiant-for-Truth from *The Pilgrim's Progress*. Having been well versed in that classic from the time he was young, Machen would likely both appreciate and humbly reject the association. Yet something can be gained by making the connection. Machen knew that the truth was not on the side of the liberals; he knew that the liberal view would not bear scrutiny. So, rather than offering hollow pronouncements condemning it, he showed it for what it was, truly lacking a place to stand either on the grounds of science and reason or on the grounds of Scripture. And in the process, he allowed the truth of Scripture to prevail.

Yet it was not only the nature of his scholarship that served to distinguish him; it was also the kind of scholarship that Machen was engaged in. Machen avoided being embroiled in the raging controversies over eschatology and Darwinism, focusing instead on issues of Christology and the doctrines of grace and the role of doctrine in the Christian faith. This is due mainly to his training—Machen was first a New Testament scholar. But it also has to do with his acuity in seeing that the issue of Christ, both his person and his work, is the central, defining issue. And on this battlefront he knew that the war was either won or lost.

A Note on the Sources

The Origin of Paul's Religion, originally published by Macmillan in 1921, has been reprinted and is currently made available by Wipf and Stock (2002). *The Virgin Birth of Christ,* also originally published by Macmillan in 1930, with a second edition appearing in 1932, was reprinted by Baker in 1967. Significant sections, even chapters in some cases, of *The Virgin Birth of Christ* first appeared in article form in the *Princeton Theological Review,* especially in the years 1905, 1906, and 1912. For a discussion of these two books, see Terry A. Chrisope, *Toward a Sure Faith* (2000), 157–71; Henry W. Coray, *J. Gresham Machen* (1981), 30–44; D. G. Hart, *Defending the Faith* (1994), 47–58, 88–91; and Ned B. Stonehouse, *J. Gresham Machen* (1987), 315–34, 462–65. For a history of critical scholarship, both in Germany and in the United States, which helps to form a backdrop for Machen's critique and contribution, see Mark A. Noll, *Between Faith and Criticism* (1986), and Roy A. Harrisville and Walter Sundberg, *The Bible in Modern Culture: Theology and Historical-Critical Method from Spinoza to Käsemann* (1995).

PART 3

MACHEN AS CITIZEN: WRITINGS ON CULTURE

While Machen's books on the New Testament and theology are well known, his writings on culture, politics, and education may not be as familiar. This section explores these areas of his thought, showing that these writings also merit our attention. We begin with an overview of Machen's engagement of the world he lived in by examining his perspective on politics and his interfacing with culture. The next chapter takes an in-depth look at just over one year in his life, from January 1918 until March 1919. This time afforded Machen an opportunity to put his thinking on politics and culture into action as he served with the YMCA during World War I. Not only was Machen an educator, he had a great deal to say about the enterprise of education, even testifying before the United States Congress on the proposed Department of Education. Chapter 9 looks at some of his thoughts on education, and also returns to the episode of the Princeton Seminary controversy and the founding of Westminster.

7

RADICALLY ETHICAL: MACHEN ON CULTURE, POLITICS, AND THE ENVIRONMENT

*This world cannot ultimately be bettered if you think
that this world is all. To move the world you must have a
place to stand.*

J. Gresham Machen, 1932

It was Abraham Kuyper who said, "There is not a square inch in the whole domain in our human existence over which Christ, who is sovereign over *all,* does not cry: 'Mine!' " And it was J. Gresham Machen who lived as if that were true. At the top of the list of Machen's favorite pastimes ranks writing letters to the editor, usually to the New York City papers, and on just about every topic imaginable. He could not resist the urge to write to senators and representatives, directors of national parks, and Philadelphia city council members. He often spoke of Christianity as being "radically ethical." And he put his belief in freedom just slightly below, if not equal to, his belief that the Bible is true. Machen played many roles: New Testament scholar, YMCA secretary, churchman, professor, administrator, author. The label of ethicist fits as well, and maybe even political activist. Yet his take on culture, politics, and the environment, like so many of his other tendencies, often led him to strange alliances and distanced him from contemporary fundamentalists. In other words, Machen forged a unique social and political philosophy. The fact that he spent so much time and energy, and wrote so much, on public and political issues may very well surprise today's readers of Machen. Exploring this area, however, reveals a significant feature of his life and thought and shows us more ways in which his legacy can affect us today.

Machen came by his interest in culture and politics honestly. His paternal grandfather, as chief clerk of the United States Senate, had more than a mild interest in politics. His father, though never giving in to the badgering to run for public office, consistently entered into political discussions and work on both local and national fronts through his roles as lawyer and engaged citizen. When Machen corresponded with his father, the three major topics were religion, books, and politics—often in that order. He also filled his letters to his brother Arthur Machen Jr. with political discussions. On his mother's side, the Greshams were also politically active; his grandfather served as mayor of Macon, Georgia, and state legislator. Though Machen never ran for public office, he carried on both family traditions as an active citizen.

His activism led him to become involved in all sorts of political issues. He wrote against the Nebraska language laws and the Lusk laws in New York, and various copyright bills and tariff laws also caught his attention. He wrote on the proposal of the Twentieth Amendment regarding child labor, and he became engaged in the discussion regarding the proposal for the Department of Education, even testifying before a joint committee of the United States Congress. Perhaps his most controversial involvement, which even spilled over into his conflict at Princeton and within the Presbyterian Church in the U.S.A., concerned his opposition to the Volstead Act and Prohibition. As H. L. Mencken wrote in the radical *American Mercury,* Machen "is a wet." These particular views are predicated on two principles governing Machen's thought: radical individual libertarianism and a particular view of the role of both the church and the individual Christian in the public arena.

But Machen was also interested in more than politics. He thought that the church and the individual Christian had much at stake in the cultural issues and battles of the day. He thought that caring about and preserving natural resources and protecting the beauty of nature even for generations to come also mattered. In the pages that follow we'll examine these aspects of Machen's thought, beginning with his view of the Christian's relationship to culture and proceeding to his politics and his views of nature and the environment.

The Christian and Culture

In one of his most reprinted essays, originally given as a commencement speech at Princeton Seminary in 1912 and published in the *Princeton Theological Review* the following year, Machen tackles "one of the greatest problems that have agitated the church," the relationship between culture and Christianity. He sketches three responses that are perennially offered as solutions to the problem. "In the first place," he writes, "Christianity may be subordinated to culture." This he sees as characterizing a great section of the church in his day. It is the tendency to accommodate Christianity to its culture. This has, unfortunately, a rich history in the Christian tradition, stretching back to the heresies of the early church, where theology was accommodated to the teachings of some of the philosophers and schools of thought or to the mystery religions of the Greco-Roman era. It also largely came to represent the ethos of the medieval period and the hegemony of the Holy Roman Empire. And "it is being favored by a very large and influential portion of the church today," notes Machen. In this view, Christianity becomes absorbed into culture, ceasing to be a supernatural religion and becoming "a human product, a mere part of human culture." The gospel and Christian teachings are no longer a check or a challenge.

The second solution goes to the other side of the pendulum, as it "seeks to destroy culture." This view "recognizes the profound evil of the world" and insulates and isolates Christianity accordingly. Taken to the extreme, this solution leads to "the abandonment of all intellectual activity" and casts aspersions on engagement in any part of human culture. Such participation is necessary, but it is "a necessary evil—a dangerous and unworthy task necessary to be gone through with under a stern sense of duty in order that thereby the higher ends of the gospel may be attained." He continues, explaining the implications, "Such men can never engage in the arts and sciences with anything like enthusiasm." Machen finds this view also in the pages of church history. The early ascetic movements of the church and medieval monasticism advocated the withdrawal from this world so that one could be unencumbered in preparing for the next. He also saw it in contemporary tendencies to decry culture and withdraw from the public arena into a Christian enclave. The problem with this approach is that it runs counter to biblical sensibilities and leads to a truncated view of God's world. As Machen notes, "The Bible, too, contains poetry that exhibits no lack of enthusiasm, no lack of a keen appreciation of beauty. With this second solution we cannot rest content." If you had to choose between these two options alone, however, Machen says that you would be better off with the second. But he holds that there is a third way.

Machen refers to the third solution to the problem of relating Christianity to culture as "consecration." Machen explains it this way:

> Instead of destroying the arts and sciences or being indifferent to them, let us cultivate them with all the enthusiasm of the veriest humanist, but at the same time consecrate them to the service of our God. Instead of stifling the pleasures afforded by the acquisition of knowledge or by the appreciation of what is beautiful, let us accept these pleasures as the gifts of a heavenly Father. Instead of obliterating the distinction between the Kingdom and the world, or on the other hand withdrawing from the world into a sort of modernized intellectual monasticism, let us go forth joyfully, enthusiastically to make the world subject to God.

This perspective does not shrink from the world on the one hand, or yield to it on the other. Echoing Kuyper's words, it provides the Christian with a newfound perspective on life and work and a newfound challenge to live out one's Christianity in the marketplace and in the art museum and in the library and in all other areas of the public arena. But it doesn't always mean, as Machen would quickly point out, that Christianity prevails. In fact, it usually does not.

This perspective also has a number of advantages. First, there is the apologetic angle. Machen notes that many of the barriers to accepting Christ are intellectual. Readily stressing the regenerative work of the Holy Spirit to overcome these obstacles, Machen also notes that "as Christians we should try to mould the thought of the world in such a way as to make the acceptance of Christianity something more than a logical absurdity." Second, Machen also notes that "modern culture is a tremendous force" affecting the lives of all classes of people. Machen indicts the church that would "simply withdraw from the conflict" as abandoning a great responsibility in light of this great challenge. Finally, this perspective has the unique ability to address the intrinsic value of the world, of human culture, and of the Christian's participation in it. Machen brings out this aspect in another writing on the thorny problem of culture, "The Christian and Human Relations." In this essay, stemming from 1915, Machen also sees three answers to the problem of the relationship of the Christian to culture, simply rewording the options he had given in his previous address. The first he refers to as the "worldly" tendency, using that word pejoratively, while the second is that of withdrawal, and the third is consecration, the same term he used earlier. He relays the difficulty of living the proposal of consecration in the sphere of human relationships, pointing to the challenge presented by relationships especially with non-Christians.

In these two essays, Machen works out his view of the consecration of culture specifically in terms of Christian scholarship and of the pastoral ministry, fitting his message to his audience, on both occasions consisting of Princeton students and faculty. Yet it would be mistaken not to see the implications of his view of the consecration of culture beyond these tasks and occupations. Machen intended his call to the consecration of culture to be heard by all Christians, and he wanted it to be exercised in all walks of life. He desired the consecration of culture broadly and actively applied in all areas of public and social life.

But here is a crucial piece of his social philosophy not to miss: he made a radical distinction between how the church collective responds and how individual Christians respond. He advocated that the church collective not become enmeshed with speaking to political issues because that tendency can easily distract from the gospel. The Christian as citizen is another matter altogether. He once wrote that the church should not be a political lobby, but added, "That does not mean at all that we deprecate advocacy of good political measures and opposition to bad measures on the part of members of the church; on the contrary we think that such activity is a very important Christian duty." He continued, stressing his commitment to individual liberty in political matters, "Christians ought to organize themselves in accordance with their consciences for the furtherance of political and social ends that they think right."

One other area of Machen's ethic needs to be addressed: in the words of D. G. Hart, Machen's commitment to the doctrine of the spirituality of the church. This commitment leads Machen to work out a different public ethic from the modernists and liberals on the one hand and from the fundamentalists on the other. He avoided the progressivism of liberalism, which identified the kingdom of God with the kingdom of this world and allowed social concerns to eclipse the gospel. He also avoided a certain triumphalism, which saw the church as manifested in its cultural power and clout, a tendency manifested in certain fundamentalist camps. Further, he avoided a defeatism, or the withdrawal from the attempt to impact culture. Instead, he advocated the distinction of the kingdom of God from this world, as opposed to progressivism. He maintained that the Christian had responsibility in the world, as counter to defeatism. And he viewed the solution to cultural woes not in wielding political power, contrary to triumphalism, but in the power of the gospel and in what he termed a "radically ethical" Christianity.

He developed this notion in an essay entitled "The Responsibility of the Church in Our New Age," first delivered before the American Academy of Political and Social Science, which invited him to address the topic in 1932. His discussion leads him to think about the nature of the new age, the postwar and by then post-Depression era, and the nature of the church. He defines the church as radically intolerant, stressing the exclusivism of the gospel and the claims of Christ; and as radically doctrinal, stressing yet again that Christianity is a religion of content. "In the third place," he adds, "the primitive church was radically ethical," which he explains as necessarily connecting the Christian life to goodness and holiness. He offers the caveats that Christians are by no means perfect and stand only in the merits of Christ and not in their own, "but they [have] been saved for holiness, and even in this life that holiness must begin to appear." He adds that the church, when true to its calling, will "be ethical in the sense that it will cherish the hope of true goodness in the other world, and that even here and now it will exhibit the beginnings of a new life which is the gift of God."

The radically ethical stance of Christianity provides Machen "a place to stand," a place from which he can speak to the culture he lives in. Machen puts it this way: "This world's problems can never be solved by those who make this world the object of their desires. This world cannot be bettered if you think that this world is all. To move the world you must have a place to stand." Machen found that place in Christianity, in the truth of the gospel. Yet he also recognized the gospel's ethical component, that the truly engaged Christian hungers and thirsts after justice and righteousness in this world and delights in seeing the world "bettered." As Machen wrote in *Christianity and Liberalism,* "[Christianity] provides fully for the social needs of mankind." Machen endeavored to live out these two foundational principles of the consecration of culture and a radically ethical Christianity. We see the fruition of those efforts in his various forays into politics and the environment and nature.

The Humdrum of Official Life

The one strand that holds Machen's divergent and per-plexing political views together consists in his bedrock view of individual liberty. Machen, while making interesting po-litical allies, always maintained a commitment to libertari-anism. "To those lovers of civil and religious liberty," he once wrote, "I confess that I belong; in fact, civil and reli-gious liberty seems to me to be more valuable than any other earthly thing." Accordingly, Machen disparaged gov-ernmental intrusion on individual liberty. He opposed the draft, instituted in World War I, even though he supported the war and served with the YMCA for over a year in France. He opposed the proposed Twentieth Amendment concerning child labor on the basis that "the amendment gives power to Congress to enter right into your home and regulate or conduct or prevent altogether the helpful work of your children without which there can be no moral de-velopment of human character." He also opposed the Vol-stead Act.

In this latter action, Machen ran afoul of his own de-nomination. Ironically, he stood alone in the New Brunswick Presbytery in his radical opposition to Harry Emerson Fosdick, the Auburn Affirmation, and the missions crisis, on the one hand, and to Prohibition, on the other. *The Philadelphia Inquirer* reported on May 12, 1926, not only that Machen was "the only one to vote against a reso-lution of [the New Brunswick Presbytery] supporting the Eighteenth Amendment," but also that Machen "is said to be the only outstanding man in the [Presbyterian] Church of a different opinion on that now burning question of the day." In fact, as the article intimates, Machen's anti-Prohibition stance hampered his getting approval by the General Assembly of the church in 1926 for his appoint-

7.1. A photograph of Machen, the mountain-climber.

ment to Princeton's apologetics chair. Though the General Assembly did not approve the appointment for other reasons, his position as a "wet" provided a convenient, ostensible reason. In the wake of such vocal and visible advocates of Prohibition as Billy Sunday and William Jennings

Bryan—who, while Secretary of State under Woodrow Wilson, ordered grape juice to be substituted for all public occasions in which he participated—Machen's position put him at odds with the fundamentalists as well.

His interest in advocating individual freedom led him to address any number of other issues, typically in the editorial pages and often in letters to politicians. One such exchange of correspondence occurred with Al Smith, four-term governor of New York and two-time contender for President of the United States. Smith was not often, if at all, commended by fundamentalists. He was Roman Catholic, and he opposed Prohibition. He found a friend in Machen. During one of his terms in office, the legislature proposed the "Lusk Teacher Laws," requiring the licensing of instructors and schools that were not public and strict controls over public ones. Machen voiced his concerns, again both in editorials and in correspondence to Smith. Smith, opposed to the laws himself, vetoed the bills that came across his governor's desk and sought the repeal of others from prior administrations. In one of the exchanges, Smith relayed to Machen, "In the humdrum of official life it is very pleasing to know that a man's efforts are appreciated."

Machen also wrote against various tariffs and copyright bills, on the principle that they infringed upon trade. And as explored further in chapter 9, he wrote against the expansion of the Bureau of Education to the Department of Education. As Machen once wrote, "Today we are rapidly becoming one of the most bureaucratic countries of the world." During the instigation of Roosevelt's New Deal programs, Machen kept busy at the typewriter writing editorials in protest. He deplored red tape and big government, opting instead for Jeffersonian principles and states' rights. In a letter to the editor printed in *The New Republic*, he declared, "We hold that the local autonomy of the States, far from being a mere matter of expediency, is at the very foundation of American freedom." Even on the local level, his concern that government not overregulate citizens' lives led him to protest the enactment of jaywalking laws by the city council of Philadelphia.

Machen also played out his public ethic in a way that further reflected his distrust of government agencies to solve social problems. This is evidenced in his longtime care of and ministry to Richard Hodges, whom Ned Stonehouse simply names as R. H. in his biography of Machen. Machen corresponded with Hodges, an alcoholic who lived in Princeton and came to Christ. And he did more than simply write to him. After Hodges became a Christian, he fell prey to his alcoholism, and on more than one occasion Machen found himself searching the streets of Princeton in the middle of the night to rescue his friend. Eventually, Machen found him a new place to stay away from the friends and temptation of his old life. He paid his rent, virtually funding the elderly and unemployed Hodges for nearly twenty years, and even paid his funeral expenses at his death. He also paid frequent visits and wrote frequent letters. And all the while, only a few knew of his efforts on Hodges's behalf. Consequently, in both private and public, Machen sought to live the "radically ethical" Christian life that he spoke of so eloquently.

Preserving Beauty

If Machen had his way, he would have been tempted to abandon his study, his books, and his career in the church and in the academy and spend his days mountain-climbing instead. His love for the mountains led him to fill his trips to Europe with frequent excursions to great slopes such as the Matterhorn. It also led him to expend a great deal of energy in trying to preserve the beauty of the mountains and of nature in his home country. He wrote against the construction of highways through the Arapaho National Forest in Colorado, and he protested the development of land in the Sequoia National Forest by the Walt Disney Corporation. But the issue that most elicited his consternation was the proposed development of roads and, in his view, the mismanagement of the land on Mt. Desert Island in Lafayette National Park.

Machen wrote in a 1920s editorial that twenty-five years before on Mt. Desert Island, "the charm of natural beauty was still unspoiled. Then," he notes, "came the federal government." While he applauds the government for protecting the land from development, he also chastises the government for its development of roads and for turning the island's natural charm "into the commonplace mold of a city park." He also wrote to the park director in the interests of curbing some of the development. In the letter, he expressed his desire "to raise the question whether the development of the park is not attended with certain dangers, which if not carefully avoided, may hinder the benefit which would otherwise accrue to our own and future generations."

Machen further spoke of how the development would "scar the mountain-side" and "injure" the views. It is also interesting to see that Machen breaks from his more typical aversion to romantic arguments in pleading on behalf of Mt. Desert Island. "The full force of the objection," Machen wrote of the case he was making, "will never be felt when it is made merely a matter of cold reasoning." He added, "If you Sir, or any lover of nature, will simply walk up through the upper part of the 'amphitheatre' or over the 'waterfall trail' on Sargent Mountain or through the beautiful woods of the Hadlock Valley between the Bubbles and Pemetic Mountain, I cannot believe that you will consign so much loveliness to destruction." He even went so far as to say that the loss of the natural beauty of

Mt. Desert Island "really seems as though some living creature were being destroyed." In the end, Machen diplomatically called for room for both those who would like to see the park developed and those who would like "to find at least a part of the Park still left in its natural state." He closed one of his many letters to the editor on the subject with similar words on behalf of those who love nature:

> There are many to whom a tree is a tree, whether artificially planted or not, and to whom a shady glen with its tangled foliage and moss-covered rocks means nothing at all. But there are also in this country some lovers of nature whose hearts are grieved. Are they altogether wrong? Must the love of nature be crushed out by Government funds? Or ought it to be cherished as a sentiment without which a people is a people with a shriveled soul? Are the national parks to be used to destroy natural beauty, or are they to conserve it for the benefit of generations yet unborn?

Though Machen disagreed with some of the policies of Theodore Roosevelt, he would have heartily agreed with the statement: "There is nothing more practical in the end than the preservation of beauty." Again, as with Machen's politics, his views on nature spring from his belief that this is God's world and that, as a Christian, he has an obligation to it. As he once wrote, "This is God's world, and those who penetrate into its secrets are students of God's works and benefactors of their fellow man."

Conclusion

This chapter merely touches the surface of Machen's engagement of culture, politics, and the environment, but it points to a significant feature of his life and thought. The next two chapters are devoted to seeing his views and theories put into action even more as he served in World War I and as he expressed his views on education. We see in these aspects of Machen's legacy that in his work as minister and as professor he cast his net wide in his service to God. Machen's response to the pressing social issues of his day might very well delight some and disappoint others. Nevertheless, there is something to be gained by his challenge to consecrate culture, to take our role as citizens seriously, even to view it as a calling. It would be much easier, as Machen himself admits, simply to avoid "the great questions." In fact, he goes even further, confessing that given the desperate nature of the situation, the minority of the Christian voice, and the countercultural claims of faith, battling with these tough questions discourages and intimidates. But as he reminds us, isolation from or accommodation to culture is not a real option for the Christian.

Consecrating culture and living a "radically ethical" Christianity in the present day meets with no less resistance than in Machen's. The ethical and social issues on the horizon are complex, and even within the church, also as in Machen's day, consensus on how to move forward is not always found. And at times the challenges appear overwhelming. But Machen, always for the underdog, offers one last word of challenge: "If we are really convinced of the truth of our message, then we can proclaim it before a world of enemies, then the very difficulty of our task, the very scarcity of our allies becomes an inspiration, then we can even rejoice that God did not place us in an easy age, but in a time of doubt and perplexity and battle."

A Note on the Sources

The two books that contain a number of Machen's essays on these issues are *The Christian Faith in the Modern World,* published in 1936, and the posthumously published *What Is Christianity? And Other Addresses,* from 1951. These crucial essays, including "The Responsibility of the Church in Our New Age" and "Christianity and Culture," along with others of interest, have been reprinted in J. Gresham Machen, *Selected Shorter Writings,* edited by D. G. Hart (2004). For discussions of Machen and culture, see Henry W. Coray, *J. Gresham Machen* (1981), 45–55; D. G. Hart, *Defending the Faith* (1994), 135–46; and Ned B. Stonehouse, *J. Gresham Machen* (1954), 400–08. Both *Understanding Fundamentalism and Evangelicalism* (1991) and *Fundamentalism and American Culture* (1980) by George Marsden provide helpful discussions of Machen within the broader context of social issues and fundamentalism. Gary Dorrien's *The Making of American Liberal Theology: Idealism, Realism, and Modernity, 1900–1950* (2003) does the same in regard to liberalism.

8

THE GREAT WAR:
MACHEN AND WORLD WAR I

Of course my feet were wet all of the time. But finally I
"salvaged" a dry pair of socks. Do you understand that
word "salvage"? It is a great word in the army. When
you see anything good lying around and appropriate it
that is not "stealing"; it is merely salvaging.

J. Gresham Machen, *"Somewhere in France,"*
October 3, 1918

In 2003, the last veteran of World War I, Jack Davis, died at the age of 108. Like Davis, the "war to end all wars" cast its long shadow over the twentieth and now the twenty-first centuries. The aftermath of that war, to which many historians have referred as the "vindictive peace," set the wheels in motion for World War II, and even the ensuing decades of the Cold War. The Arab region, plagued by conflict throughout the twentieth century, was still reeling from the breakup of the Ottoman Empire and the creation of the various Gulf region states, one of the many far-flung effects of the Allies' contest with the Central Powers. The war itself wreaked havoc and desolation from 1914 to 1918 while it tore through the heart of Europe. Close to eight million lost their lives in the war, with France alone losing almost one and a half million of a population of thirty-six million. One had to go to great lengths to find someone not directly affected by the war. When America became involved, the army, hovering around 120,000 or so, ballooned to four and a half million, both from volunteers and from the newly instituted draft. Machen, well past the reaches of the draft board, wanted to do his part. "It is a sense of duty," he wrote, "that impels me." Eventually, he went with the YMCA, serving French troops and the American Expeditionary Forces (A.E.F.), leaving from New York City at the end of January 1918 onboard a steamer ship and returning March 2, 1919.

His letters from this period disclose that the war had a profound impact on his life. He returned from the war with a keen sense of purpose and a deep-seated commitment. The war no less impacted his theology. He had witnessed firsthand both the darkest side of humanity and also the brightest. He saw both utter disregard for life and true, selfless sacrifice, sometimes nearly simultaneously. He learned, in other words, the deeper reality of the doctrines of total depravity and of common grace. He once wrote that "it is not always easy to carry this work of consecration [of culture]"—his perspective on the Christian's proper relationship to culture, as we saw in the previous chapter. His service in France and Belgium during this long, hard year would indeed be one of those times. It served as a catalyst, if not for the forming, then at least for the galvanizing of his theology and his understanding of the Christian's relationship to culture. The war had no less impact on his contemporaries and their theology as well. Below we will explore Machen's work with the YMCA "over there," as the words from one of the many songs stemming from the Great War put it. We will also examine the impact of the war on the theology of Machen and his contemporaries. But first we look at why Machen, and America for that matter, went to war at all.

From Princeton to Paris

Even though he had been on the faculty at Princeton Seminary for a decade and had received attention in larger circles for his limited but significant publications, Machen was restless in the middle years of the 1910s, perhaps the same restlessness he had experienced after his undergraduate work. Too soon to be called a midlife crisis, the struggle in Machen's mid-thirties was with a desire to be "useful," a word often occurring in his correspondence from this period. When war first broke out in Europe in 1914, Machen shared the sentiment of much of the nation to keep out of the war. Woodrow Wilson himself was reelected in 1916 largely on the slogan, "He kept us out of war." Events quickly unfolded—the sinking of the *Lusitania* and the famous "Zimmerman Telegram" among them—that changed the nation's neutrality to a declaration of war on Germany on April 6, 1917.

Machen reflects both the initial ambivalence and the later change in his own view on the war. Having spent a delightful time in Germany, Machen was much impressed by the German nation and had his suspicions of Britain's motives, which he saw largely revolving around trade interests. In fact, in 1914 he wrote, "The alliance of Great Britain with Russia and Japan seems to me still an unholy thing—an unscrupulous effort to crush the life out of a progressive commercial rival." Yet as the war progressed, he also saw that Germany moved beyond the mere protection of its interests, being encircled by the Triple Entente powers of France,

Britain, and Russia, to a more aggressive campaign of invasion. He applauded Wilson's "Peace without Victory" speech in January 1917, calling for an end to the seemingly endless war. But as those crucial spring months unfolded, Machen threw himself into support of the war, writing on April 7, the day after war was declared by Congress, "I feel as though I ought to have some immediate part in the manifold work that is going forward." The "manifold work" consisted of the various components of mobilizing a nation for war. What Machen longed to do most of all was minister to soldiers, and he spent the next few months figuring out how best to do so.

He considered the chaplaincy first, ruling it out on the basis that he felt inadequate—"I believe I should be terribly footless as a chaplain" was how he put it—and because he thought the chaplains, who were de facto officers, could not empathize with the enlisted men. He also, like so many others, looked into serving as an ambulance driver. He was advised, however, that there was every chance that once in Europe he would be assigned to munitions loading and transport instead, again leaving him without the contact with soldiers that he desired. In the end, he felt that he would be most useful in the YMCA. He began his work holding church services and preaching in training camps before being sent to Paris to await his assignment. A letter sent just before he embarked reveals a certain anxiety. Boarding the ship days before he left, he waited, wondering what might lie ahead.

The Sign of the Red Triangle

Machen wore the YMCA uniform, along with approximately 26,000 other volunteers, and he operated one of almost five hundred "huts" or canteens serving soldiers on

8.1. Transportation Orders during Machen's YMCA service in World War I.

the front lines. The YMCA carried on any number of duties. It was an educational institution for soldiers, many of whom had merely a grammar-school education. As a precursor to the USO, the YMCA provided entertainment, mostly in the spirit and style of vaudeville, for the troops. It ran hostels in the leave areas for soldiers, providing them a place to stay, meals, and at times a protective hedge from the temptations of the city streets. But perhaps what the servicemen appreciated above all were the huts or canteens, operated literally within shooting distance of the front lines and sometimes situated in the trenches themselves. General John Pershing, commander of the U.S. troops during the war, credited the YMCA for conducting 90 percent of the humanitarian and welfare work for American and Allied forces. The telltale sign of the YMCA was the upside-down red triangle, a sign that brought joy to any soldier—or, as one soldier put it, "the last evidence that anybody cares." Machen spent most of his time during the war operating one of these huts, or a Foyer, for French soldiers. As an international effort, the YMCA served beyond the needs of American troops. Given Machen's ability to speak French, he made a perfect candidate for this service.

The YMCA hut filled many needs. Since World War I, the army itself has developed units and programs to meet the social needs of soldiers, but in World War I, the YMCA performed those duties. The hut was home to soldiers quite far geographically and otherwise from the comforts of the ones they had left; it was a library offering reading materials to distract, even if for a moment, from the horrors of the war; it was a theater offering a respite of entertainment; and it was a church. Those who manned the huts, each one typically run by one YMCA worker dubbed a "secretary," provided soldiers with writing paper and pens—and sometimes even postage—so that soldiers could keep in touch with their families; sent money orders, which was a virtual lifeline for some families back home; kept a supply of magazines and books to be lent out; and sold cups of hot tea and hot chocolate by the thousands at cost. On one day alone, Machen served 1,200 cups of hot chocolate from his hut—at a time long before instant cocoa.

All supplies had to be accounted for and ordered by the secretary, who also made all the hot chocolate, served it, and recorded all the financial transactions. The work began before the doors of the hut opened and continued after they had closed, and the doors were open ten to twelve hours a day. Not surprisingly, a private in the 19th Regiment of Engineers, serving "somewhere in France," wrote, "The Y.M.C.A. man is a very busy man and of the ones I have come in contact with [I] have always found them willing to help whenever they had the opportunity."

The Sinister Buzz

Expecting to be assigned to specifically religious work, conducting worship services, preaching, leading Bible studies, and offering pastoral counseling, Machen viewed his assignment to run a hut for French soldiers with disappointment, but only initially. Though his work was monotonous and sometimes surprisingly uneventful, Machen took to it. He was first assigned at St. Mard, an area near Soissons, about fifty miles northwest of Paris. This area had been the site of intense fighting and even of a significant mutiny involving numerous divisions of French soldiers in the earlier years of the war. By the spring of 1918, the village of St. Mard lay devastated, simply held by the Allies and not the scene of fighting on the ground, leaving scores of rats as the only enemy to contend with. The nights, however, were made "hideous . . . by the sinister buzz of the German planes on their way to some work of destruction," and the days were filled with the rancor of guns and explosions from battles in the near distance. "I feel as though it would be a relief to the eyes," Machen wrote, "to see a window-pane once more, and a relief to the ears *not* to hear at intervals the noise of guns and distant shells."

He was transferred to Missy, across the Aisne River and a few miles closer to the front than Soissons. It was a significant location along a major military highway, making it a very active place with perpetual and unforgettable scenes of migration of displaced and barely surviving peasants from the countryside and processions of wounded and dead sol-

8.2. A letter from J. Gresham Machen to his mother, July 22, 1918. Machen refers to a hasty move, in which he lost some of his gear, shopping for supplies for the YMCA Hut, visiting the evacuation hospital, and "having a thorough test made of my gas-masks."

diers. And Machen was busy at work in the Foyer. "I have worn one uniform ever since leaving Paris. And it is now all spotted up with hot chocolate," he wrote. The planes and shells were relentless overhead, leading him to write of "the concussion of the air," adding, "It is rather a brutal violation of the two elements, earth and air. I hate it, as I hate the whole business of war. But I am convinced that in the interests of peace the allies have simply got to win."

His service at Missy came to an abrupt end near the close of May. He, along with the troops stationed there, barely escaped with his life—leaving behind everything except the uniform on his back—as the city was utterly destroyed, and he crossed the bridge over the Aisne River moments before the German army demolished it. It was a most exciting time as Machen spent two days merely one step ahead of the advancing German troops and the wake of destruction, writing, "The scenes that I have witnessed can never be forgotten, but it is not so easy to make anyone else realize what they were like." His family, now including nieces, nephews, and sisters-in law in addition to his mother and brothers, heard news of the German advance in Baltimore and suffered through an intense few weeks without receiving mail from Machen and fearing the worst. When the cable arrived bearing the message "Safe and well," a home in Baltimore celebrated.

He returned to Paris, where he was reassigned to work with the 37th Division of the American Expeditionary Forces. Now his duties expanded to include preaching and leading Bible studies among the troops in addition to pouring out the refreshing cups of hot chocolate, ministering to both body and soul. Machen's duties left him with but three or four hours of sleep a day. The 37th Division, made up mostly of the National Guard from Ohio, participated in the biggest operation of the American forces in the war, the

Meuse-Argonne offensive. Occurring in the final weeks of the war, the offensive aimed at capturing the hub of the German railroad, cutting off supplies and, as it turned out, hastening the armistice and the end of the war. Machen went with the troops as they trudged through the densely fortified Argonne Forest. Machen now spent a great deal of time working in the dressing stations, serving the wounded—both Americans and captured Germans. And here he witnessed remarkable signs of humanity amid the terrors of war, as this selection from a letter relating his activities at the dressing station reveals:

> One German fellow said when I gave him the chocolate that it was "wie bei der Mutter." It would have taken a harder heart than mine to keep from being touched by that. By the way, along with the hatred and bitterness incidental to war, there are some examples of the other thing which like the fair lilies in swampy ground are all the more beautiful because of the contrast with the unlikely soil in which they grow. Thus at one of the dressing stations near the front, I saw an American wounded soldier deliberately take off his overcoat and give it to a wounded German who was suffering a lot worse than he. When one reflects what that little act meant—the long cold hours of rain and damp along the way to the rear and the interminable waits—it becomes clear that magnanimity has not altogether perished from the earth.

Machen was also moved by the ruin of the countryside, "a scene of desolation so abominable." He adds, "I have seen burnt and ruined forests before. But the effects of shell-fire are different. There was something indescribably sinister about the scene of ruin." He had more of the countryside to see than he wanted to as they fought their way through France and into Belgium. A month or so before the end of the war, he wrote that his "shoes gave out completely under the stress" of the marching, adding, "Of course my feet were wet all the time." He recalls what happened next:

> But finally I "salvaged" a dry pair of socks. Do you understand that word "salvage"? It is a great word in the army. When you see anything good lying around and appropriate it that is not "stealing"; it is merely salvaging. . . . You may laugh, and think I am irreverent, but I can say in all seriousness that one of the most fervent prayers that I ever offered in my life was the prayer of thanksgiving that I prayed that night in my dug-out when I pulled on those warm socks.

Danger was also constantly close at hand. He records that while he was walking with a few soldiers, "a shell burst a few feet from us, we beat a retreat, seeking the comparative shelter of ditches and shell holes." And at times his duties consisted of acting as a stretcher-bearer, "burying the dead, and spending the nights in shell-holes." One time, because of his ability in French, he was tasked by a lieutenant to select from a great crowd of refugees the most needy who could be transported out quickly in the limited space of an ambulance. Reflecting on the horrors of the duty, he wrote, "Can you imagine a more pathetic task? It was like the last boat-load leaving the Titanic." He shoved and crowded as many as he could into the ambulance—"It was *some* wagonload, I can tell you," he wrote. He later reflected on what he had learned through these most trying times:

> Out in the dressing station, when the shells were falling close around, I somehow gained the conviction that I was in God's care and He would not try me beyond my strength; that courage would keep pace with danger, or rather that danger (for I confess it turned out rather that way) would keep within the limits of courage. In short, I understand the eighth chapter of Romans better.

Peace at last, praise to God!

On the eleventh hour of the eleventh day of the eleventh month in 1918, the war came to an end. The night before, on November 10, Machen had been on the front without a firm sense that the end of the war was near, as he wrote in a letter to his mother: "Little news had been coming through about the progress of negotiations," adding, "Without a doubt you were far better and far more promptly informed in Baltimore." The constant rumors of the war's end had disappointed Machen so much that he had just about given up hope. When it was finally over, however, he could not contain his joy and praise, exclaiming:

> The Lord's Name be praised! Hardly before have I known what true thanksgiving is. Nothing but the exuberance of the Psalms of David accompanied with the psaltery on an instrument of ten strings could begin to do justice to the joy of this hour. "Bless the Lord, O my soul." It seems to me as though the hills must break forth into singing. Peace at last, and praise to God!

Bells rang out everywhere and celebration filled the air. Yet after months of relentless shelling, gunfire, air raids, and the sounds of destruction, Machen reveled in the silence, as he wrote, "But we heard something greater by far—in contrast with the familiar roar of war—namely the silence of that misty morning. I think I can venture upon the paradox. That was a silence that could really be heard. I suppose it was the most eloquent, the most significant silence in the history of the world." Machen's work would last another four months before he was to return to Princeton.

With the war over, Machen's duties shifted. He could now devote more time to preaching, something he had been wanting to do all along. And he largely served as an itinerant preacher in the various camps around Paris from December 1918 through March 1919. The YMCA was deeply involved in the debriefing and "repatriation" process in bringing the soldiers back home. Additionally, significant troops remained after the armistice. Machen, quite missing his academic environs, also took advantage of the time to sit in on lectures with the various French luminaries in biblical studies and theology. At one point when he first began his service, he wrote, "You don't know how I long for home these days." On March 2, 1918, his wishes were realized as Machen returned home to joyful reunions with his family and his Princeton colleagues.

The Church and the War

Many intellectuals and clergy served in a similar capacity to Machen during the war. Yet the war did not have a uniform impact on those who witnessed its horrors firsthand. Ernest Hemingway served in the ambulance corps, even writing about his experiences and perspective on war in *A Farewell to Arms* (1929) and on the postwar generation, the so-called "Lost Generation," in *The Sun Also Rises* (1926). Harry Emerson Fosdick also served in the war as an ambulance driver and a chaplain. Fosdick's brother Raymond Fosdick served in a prominent role as head of the Committee on Training Camp Activities. The YMCA actually functioned under the auspices of the committee, which oversaw, among other things, even the huts like the one Machen ran. Handpicked by U.S. Secretary of War Newton Baker, Raymond Fosdick, quite the moral reformer, ran an ambitious campaign to keep the American soldiers morally upright during their time far away from home and surrounded by temptation.

It might be hard to explain Harry Emerson Fosdick's rather high view of humanity as naturally good that permeates his theology in light of his experiences in the war. We would assume that he would have become much more committed to the doctrine of original sin after going through war rather than, as was the case, reject the doctrine altogether. Yet in many ways, Fosdick represents the irony of postwar America. In the Roaring Twenties, the horrors of the war served as only a vague and distant memory. Perhaps aided by distance and the separation of an ocean, America in the 1920s experienced an explosion of optimism; indeed, the progressive era, begun in the 1910s, met only a speed bump in the tenure of the Great War.

This, of course, is not true of all. Hemingway is a good example of one who faced the realities of the war and the postwar era in all their desperation. Sigmund Freud, Margaret Mead, the "flapper generation," and the independence-creating automobile were all contributing to a paradigm shift in the nation's morality, leaving the lost generation to pay little heed to the voices of either liberals or fundamentalists. Curiously, Machen's outlook resonated more with Hemingway's than Fosdick's, though of course he could neither share the extent of Hemingway's despair nor accept it as the ultimate response.

Machen's references to the war in his writings, excepting his letters, do not add up to much. That is not to say, however, that it had little impact on his thought. First, it cemented his life's ambition, which had been only loosely in place before the war. Machen returned on the steamer with a newfound devotion to his life as New Testament scholar, with the requisite commitment enabling him to persevere as the spokesperson for theological conservatism through years of controversy. Second, the war affected his theology, perhaps best demon-

8.3. A photograph of Machen in his YMCA uniform, c. 1918.

strated in an address given before Princeton alumni just after he returned entitled, "The Church in the War."

This brief address does not concern the justness of the war or the debate over pacifism or military involvement, offering instead a discussion of the gospel. On this count, he charges that the church failed "because men have been unwilling to receive, and the church has been unwilling to preach, the gospel of Christ crucified." He explains, "The leading characteristic of the present age is a profound satisfaction with human goodness," citing the war literature as "redolent of such satisfaction." He attributes this tendency to the notion that times of war offer such a great opportunity to see the sins of others that one's own sins go unnoticed. He also sees that "the sense of sin has sometimes been blunted by the consciousness of the great achievement." Above all, however, this attitude was due to an unbridled belief in human ability, which, having germinated long before the war, was coming into full flower. Christianity, conversely, "is the religion of the brokenhearted." It requires the conviction of sin; it requires the preaching of the cross.

Machen acknowledges that it smacks of "a colossal piece of impertinence" to fling about in the celebrations of the war victory and its innumerable stories of heroism and achievement. He shared in those celebrations, but he never lost sight of humanity's true need, and he would not substitute valor on the battlefield for the cloak of Christ's righteousness. He pulled back from the optimism that overflowed in the thought of his liberal counterparts because he could not extinguish the necessity of keeping the gospel central to the mission of the church, both in times of war and in times of victory and peace. This approach stands in stark contrast to Harry Emerson Fosdick's dictum, "The missionary enterprise is the Christian campaign for international good will." Perhaps on this point more than on any other, the true difference between liberalism and theological conservatism becomes patently obvious.

This is not to suggest that Machen neglected the pressing social issues either during or after the war. In *Christianity and Liberalism,* he spoke of the fundamentalist tendency to minister to the individual soul while liberalism addressed the social ills. Machen, as he often did in his engagement with culture, forged a middle way, claiming, "Though Christianity is individualistic, it is not only individualistic. It provides fully for the social needs of man." Indeed, during the war, he declared, "If this war is ever concluded in a really satisfactory way, I am going to be an active worker for peace."

Perhaps most instructive from Machen's response to the war concerns not only the way he avoided the optimism of liberalism, but also the way he deflected the despair so prevalent in the lost generation. The familiar and reliable beliefs in God and country and the sense that the world held purpose and meaning, and even beauty, fell away as a significant swath of that young generation fell adrift. They felt their alienation and dire need acutely. But they did not see the redemptive and restorative power of the gospel that Machen also wrote of in "The Church in the War." Stressing the inability and lostness of humanity due to sin, he also proclaimed that at the cross, "sin is dealt with once for all, and then a new and a joyous life follows," and that from the cross, "the Christian may now proceed without fear." This was the message of hope that Machen proclaimed. That hope was not to be found in the "deeds of goodness of the millions of the human race." Neither was it to be crushed by the countless acts of horror just unleashed on the world.

Conclusion

A picture of Machen's humanity comes through when we see him excited over a pair of dry socks and gleefully, with all the energy of a child at Christmastime, putting them on and having for the first time in many days a good night's sleep. We see his compassion as he stands in the hut in his hot-chocolate-stained uniform handing over cup after cup to the war-weary soldiers. And we see his sense of the great human cost of the war as he stands by the side of the soldiers at the dressing stations and watches the miles of refugees, which, for him, "constituted the saddest part of all." This is not the mere two-dimensional figure who comes to us in the pages of *Christianity and Liberalism* or *The Virgin Birth of Christ*. We can move beyond our picture of

Machen as the consummate scholar, denizen of Old Princeton, and central defender of theological conservatism.

New challenges faced Machen as he returned home and stood at the onset of the 1920s. These would not be the challenges of dodging nearby exploding shells, or of trying to wrest a few moments of sleep while planes buzzed overhead, or of considering what words to say while ministering to wounded soldiers. He learned much from the war, nevertheless, that would help him face the challenges lying ahead. Quite early in his service, he pledged, "If God will I may return to the preaching of the gospel with new appreciation of the privileges." One can scarcely imagine the urgent circumstances accompanying that pledge. But one can easily see his commitment to it in the years to come.

A Note on the Sources

The letters of Machen are in the Machen Archives, Montgomery Library, Westminster Theological Seminary. "The Church in the War" has been reprinted in J. Gresham Machen, *Selected Shorter Writings,* edited by D. G. Hart (2004). For discussions of Machen and World War I, see D. G. Hart, *Defending the Faith* (1994), 45–47, and Ned B. Stonehouse, *J. Gresham Machen* (1954), 240–303. Stonehouse reprints a number of Machen's war letters. See Harry Emerson Fosdick's, *The Challenge of the Present Crisis* (1917), for his wartime "message" to America. For a concise treatment of World War I, see Michael Howard, *The First World War* (2002). For the impact of the war on American culture, including religion, see Meirion and Susie Harries, *The Last Days of Innocence: America at War, 1917–1918* (1997), and Robert H. Zieger, *America's Great War: World War I and the American Experience* (2000).

9

SOLID LEARNING: MACHEN ON EDUCATION

It is very encouraging to find a minister who does not believe that the cultivation of the intellect is at all hostile to pastoral service.

J. Gresham Machen, November 15, 1924

Fifty years ago many colleges and universities and theological seminaries were devoted to the truth of God's Word. But one by one they have drifted away. . . .

J. Gresham Machen, September 25, 1929

Perhaps the most well-known portrait of Machen, currently gracing a fireplace mantel in Machen Hall at Westminster Seminary, depicts him as the consummate academic, clad in his doctoral robe and hood, with papers and books on his desk. There is a softness and warmth to his expression, his hair is graying, and all the while he appears content and comfortable in his role and in his life's occupation. This portrait, painted in the 1930s, captures Machen the scholar. There was a time, however, when he was not such a serious student. He kept his notebooks from his seminary days at Princeton, and they are quite revealing. In addition to dutifully taking notes, he also demonstrated a proclivity for doodling. He practiced his penmanship and his German, writing "Ich bin krank," among other phrases, again and again. He even took advantage of writing notes, in large bold letters, to his classmates, from "GOOD BYE MUNSON," to the more exhortatory "DON'T HORSE PARKE," and "TAKE NOTES DUDLEY!" You would have to look hard at the portrait of Machen the scholar to see the glimmer of Machen the student goofing off by writing notes during lectures. But to understand Machen on education and as an educator—encompassing his testifying before Congress on the proposed Department of Education to the pouring of his very being into the formation of Westminster Seminary—you must start with Machen as a Princeton Seminary student, even one who doodles during lectures on church history. In fact, you must go back even further to his days at Johns Hopkins and to his boyhood years on West Monument Street in Baltimore.

While Machen never wrote a book on education, his writings on the subject could easily fill one or even a few volumes. This chapter explores this area of Machen's writings, which include his testimony before the United States Congress, his various essays on the nature and task of Christian scholarship, and his thoughts on a philosophy of education, specifically the education of ministers. This chapter also affords an opportunity to revisit the Princeton Seminary controversy and the formation of Westminster Theological Seminary. That controversy turned largely on doctrine, but it also concerned the role that the teaching of doctrine played in the business of educating ministers. Given that Machen was involved in higher education from the time he entered Johns Hopkins in 1898 until his death in 1937, his role as educator factors significantly in his life and thought. It also provides a number of ideas that merit our attention in the twenty-first century. We will begin with Princeton and the trajectory of rigorous intellectual training for ministry that Machen became a part of and then took with him to Philadelphia in 1929. Next follows a look at Machen's thought on public education, ending with his model of a truly lifelong learner.

Solid Learning

Sensing the need for a seminary to train ministers, the Presbyterian Church at the 1811 General Assembly laid the groundwork for Princeton Theological Seminary. In addition to setting aside funds, the assembly also established the mission statement or the "plan" for the institution. This plan posed a difficult task for the fledgling school in that it committed itself to uniting what often gets divided asunder. In short, it sought union of intellect and religious devotion, of faith and learning, or, as the plan proposed, "solid learning." The plan put it this way: the seminary would bring together "that piety of the heart which is the fruit only of the renewing and sanctifying grace of God, with solid learning; believing that religion without learning, or learning without religion, in the ministers of the gospel, must ultimately prove injurious to the church." In 1812, the same year that the young nation was at war with Britain, Princeton Theological Seminary began its quest to fulfill that plan. In the years that followed, some of the most capable theologians of American religious history, such as Charles Hodge and B. B. Warfield, saw to it that those words were not merely carved in granite, but that they pulsed through the life of the institution. In 1912, on the occasion of the seminary's hundredth anniversary, then president Francis Patton spoke of Princeton's theology accurately, though humorously: "In the centuries to come, should the theological paleontologist dig it up and pay attention to it, he will be constrained to say that it at least belonged to the order of vertebrates."

In the nineteenth century, especially in American higher education, the noble goals of Princeton were not unique. Education for the professions (there weren't many beyond the clergy, law, and medicine) largely entailed a good dose of the classics, languages, literature, and theology. Even undergraduate programs by and large weighed heavily toward the liberal-arts side of the curriculum. Much of the practical preparation for the professions came in apprenticeships, taking a slim margin of the curriculum. This changed a great deal with the turn of the twentieth century, which brought an increased emphasis on practical matters. Machen, as well as many others, often attributed the shift to the onset of pragmatism. Regardless of the source, the push was on for a more practical curriculum, and Princeton Theological Seminary was not immune. It is probably no mere coincidence that Machen's chief antagonist among the faculty at Princeton was Charles Erdman, professor of practical theology.

Much is often made of the Princeton controversy's hinging largely on personalities. Machen, on the one side, is often depicted as belligerent and cantankerous, not a team player. Erdman, and his ally president J. Ross Stevenson, are portrayed as the placaters, as the diplomatic peacemakers. There may be something to this. Charles Erdman, by many counts, was the quintessential gentleman—although he could be unscrupulous to Machen on occasion. And it is true that Machen could be somewhat pugilistic if he wished. But the issues at stake, as earlier chapters have demonstrated, were not nonessential. Machen could be every part the gentleman, but the occasion called for more than diplomacy. Consequently, it was not personalities at odds; it was a matter of opposing positions that were deeply and widely apart. Erdman and Stevenson thought the seminary should represent the broader spectrum of the denomination, not just the slice of theological conservatives. Consequently, they were in favor of appointments to the board—and eventually to the faculty—of signers of the Auburn Affirmation. This approach simply mirrored Erdman's practice while serving as moderator of the General Assembly in 1925, appointing signers of the Auburn Affirmation to chair key committees.

But something else was brewing at Princeton besides these clashes and significant theological differences: the emergence of a fundamentally different approach to ministerial preparation from what had long held sway. Machen saw it coming, and he also saw that it was bound up with the doctrinal slide. Fulfilling the words of the seminary's original plan, the failure to maintain both intellectual rigor and religious devotion together in educating ministers "must ultimately prove injurious to the church." This is not to suggest that Machen disdained what counts for practical theology in seminary curricula, nor does it suggest that Machen favored only the stuffy academic in the pulpit lecturing congregations right up to the brink of boredom. He opposed such preaching, and he did so strongly. Yet he viewed the task of preaching as a sacred trust and the opening of God's Word as monumental, not at all to be taken lightly.

Machen's contention with Erdman had nothing to do with practical theology. Machen insisted, in concert with Princeton's original plan, on that half of the equation in the training of ministers. What he feared, and saw in Erdman, was the potential of the emphasis on practical theology to swallow up the other half of the equation. More specifically, Machen's contention with Erdman had everything to do with Erdman's philosophy of education, which, given Erdman's influence in training a generation of ministers, alarmed Machen as to the future prospects for the church. Erdman did not stress knowledge of or extensive studies in the original Greek and

Hebrew languages of the Bible. He also favored reducing the number of classes in biblical and theological studies in order to make more room for practical courses. In short, he proposed weakening Princeton's reputed backbone.

It is interesting to see Machen's response to these pressures. He developed his view over time. As a fairly young and more recent faculty member at Princeton, Machen had actually favored a curriculum revision that would make room for more electives and reduce biblical studies courses. The other side was represented by B. B. Warfield, who in the interim between Francis Patton's retirement and J. Ross Stevenson's appointment acted as president of the seminary, and who favored a more traditional curriculum of required courses and a minimum of practical courses. Later, in the 1920s, Machen realized the dangers that this curriculum shift presented, so he became solidly committed to maintaining the standard of Princeton's rigorous approach to ministerial preparation and came to see the virtues of Warfield's position. In the process, he found himself at odds with the president, Stevenson, and one of the most popular faculty members, Erdman. That, coupled with the tolerance of liberalism, led to his rift from Princeton. In earlier chapters we explored the theological issues concerning the Princeton controversy. It is also helpful in understanding Machen to see the educational philosophy issues of that controversy. Two of Machen's shorter writings in particular offer his thoughts on a philosophy of seminary education and ministerial preparation: his address on the opening of Westminster Seminary and a short series of lectures given before the Bible League in Caxton Hall, Westminster, London.

The Importance of Christian Scholarship

Machen received numerous invitations not only to teach at other institutions, but also to be president. The trustees

9.1. Portrait of J. Gresham Machen, 1937, Machen Hall, Westminster Theological Seminary.

of both Cedarville College of Ohio and the newly established college named for the famed prosecutor in the Scopes Monkey Trial in Dayton, Tennessee, Bryant College, invited him to be president. Lewis Sperry Chafer, upon hearing that Machen was leaving Princeton, even invited him to Dallas Theological Seminary, then named Evangelical Theological College. But Machen could not bring himself to leave Princeton. When he was finally forced out, he also could not bring himself to leave behind Princeton's noble tradition of education. Consequently, in founding Westminster Theological Seminary, he clearly intended for it to carry on the tradition of solid learning from Old Princeton.

After a very busy summer of planning, Westminster began in the fall of 1929 with both breakaway students and faculty from Princeton. Machen delivered the opening address on September 25, 1929. Toward the end of his remarks, he lamented, "Fifty years ago many colleges and universities and theological seminaries were devoted to the truth of God's Word. But one by one they have drifted away, often with all sorts of professions of orthodoxy on the part of those who were responsible for the change." Unfortunately, as Machen saw it, Princeton qualified for that category as well, and he cited as evidence both the appointment of signers of the Auburn Affirmation to the board and the silence of other board members in the face of that action. Then he declared, "Though Princeton Seminary is dead, the noble tradition of Princeton Seminary is alive."

He meant that the tradition is alive not only in terms of doctrine and principle, but also in its original commitment to fusing piety and solid learning. Such a commitment, he pledged, would thrive at Westminster. These closing words were preceded by his discussion of the purpose and curriculum of the new seminary. "Specialists in the Bible—that is what Westminster Seminary will endeavor to produce," served as the purpose, accomplished by a regimen of biblical studies, with emphasis on Greek and Hebrew, biblical theology, systematic theology, church history, and practical theology, though he added that much of what counts for practical theology is not learned within the walls of a seminary, but on the job, "by the long experience of subsequent years." The focus would be on biblical studies and exegesis, as he explained, "If the students of our seminary can read the Bible not merely in translations, but as it was given [in the original languages] by the Holy Spirit to the church, then they are prepared to deal intelligently with the question of what the Bible means." The result, according to

Machen, is a graduate who is a minister with a message, and "who can so deliver his message as to reach the hearts and minds of men." He filled his opening address with inspiring rhetoric: "We believe that a theological seminary is an institution of higher learning whose standards should not be inferior to the highest academic standards that anywhere prevail"; "Our message is based, indeed, directly upon the Bible"; and "If you want men who know the Bible and who know it in something more than a layman's sort of way, then call on us. If we can give you such men, we have succeeded; if we cannot give them to you, we have failed." Yet when you understand the struggle out of which Machen had just come at Princeton as forming the backdrop for these words, they become more than mere rhetoric. They express the heart of Machen's understanding of seminary education.

He demonstrates the necessity of such rigorous training not only in the model of his own experience with battling liberalism in the Presbyterian Church and at Princeton, but also in his thoughts in a 1932 series of lectures he delivered in London for the meetings of the Bible League. He begins those lectures by deploring the current state of education, noting, "Modern pedagogy has emancipated us, whether we be in the pulpit or in the professor's chair or in the pew, from anything so irksome as earnest labour in the acquisition of knowledge." He then refers to the ascendancy of methodology, observing, "It never seems to occur to many modern teachers that the primary business of the teacher is to study the subject that he is going to teach. Instead of studying the subject that he is going to teach, he studies 'education'; a knowledge of the methodology of teaching takes the place of the particular branch of literature, history, or science to which a man has devoted his life."

Machen then draws attention to the impact of this educational trend on the church. The emphasis on methodol-

9.2. Westminster Seminary students at work in the library in the seminary's first location on Pine Street, Philadelphia, early 1930s.

ogy in both Christian education and ministerial preparation runs counter to the great emphasis on content that Machen sees as the pressing need of the hour. The biblical revelation is by and large content, "the body of truth which God has revealed." Once we see this, Machen contends, "we shall regard it as our supreme function as teachers and as preachers and as Christian parents and as simple Christians to impart a knowledge of the body of truth." Consequently, the fuller our understanding of that knowledge, the fuller our work will be. Far from being isolated from the Christian life, Christian scholarship occupies its core.

He proceeds to sketch the three areas in which Christian scholarship is necessary: evangelism, the defense of the faith, and the building up of the body of Christ—things to which all Christians, at various levels, are called. He admits that the reference to evangelism might surprise some, and that its importance might be flatly denied by some, especially those who pit faith against knowledge. Yet, as Machen points out, "Faith always contains an intellectual element," for there is, in terms of Christian faith, the knowledge of Christ's person and work. He also argues that while not all evangelists are scholars, "scholarship is necessary to evangelism all the same," noting that Paul and Martin Luther, among the greatest of the evangelists, were scholars and adding that "evangelists who are not scholars are dependent upon scholars to help them get their message straight; it is out of a great underlying fund of Christian learning that true evangelism springs." He also returns to one of the themes of *Christianity and Liberalism,* stating, "Life, according to the New Testament, is founded upon truth." Consequently, he challenges the one who offers only a personal testimony as the sum of evangelism. "We shall be poor witnesses," he declares, "if we recount only the experiences of our own lives." Instead, "we must preach to them the Lord Jesus Christ."

This naturally leads to his second point, the defense of the faith. Again in keeping with the tradition of Old Princeton, Machen argues, "A Christianity that avoids argument is not the Christianity of the New Testament." Of course, he acknowledges that "argument alone is quite insufficient to make a man a Christian," and emphasizes the necessity of the Holy Spirit in bringing true conviction. Nevertheless, especially given the encroachment of modernism, to which he draws attention, the intellectual atmosphere is not conducive to Christianity. Rather than sound retreat, Machen calls for "Christian scholars to meet the attack." People are rejecting Christianity, Machen observes, simply because they believe it's not true, to which Machen replies, "The Christian religion flourishes not in the darkness, but in the light. Intellectual slothfulness is but a quack remedy for unbelief; the true remedy is consecration of intellectual powers to the service of the Lord Jesus Christ." But the defense of the faith not only is oriented to those outside of the church, but also includes those inside, a point made more pertinent given Machen's context. He challenged his audience in London accordingly: "A return to solid instruction in the pulpit, at the desk of the Sunday school teacher, and particularly in the home is one of the crying needs of the hour." At the center of that instruction is the Bible, as he states, "What a world in itself the Bible is, my friends! Happy are those who in the providence of God can make the study of it very specifically the business of their lives, but happy also is every Christian who has it open before him and seeks by daily study to penetrate somewhat into the wonderful richness of what it contains."

Not only did he share this vision of Christian scholarship with the Bible League in London, he also inculcated it into the lives of his students at Princeton and Westminster. Many of them looked to Machen both while under his teaching and afterward while serving in their ministries. His voluminous correspondence includes scores of letters exchanged with his former students. One of them was pastoring a church in Blackey, Kentucky, when he sought Machen's advice on where to find information on the Apocrypha. Machen wrote back, answering his question and updating him on things at Princeton. He also passed along these comments: "I am delighted to hear about the splendid way in which your work is progressing. It is very encouraging to find a minister who does not believe that the cultivation of the intellect is at all hostile to pastoral service." He gave the same thoughts to another former student, Harold John Ockenga. Ockenga, before he went on to be pastor of Park Street Church in Boston and president of both Fuller and Gordon-Conwell Theological Seminaries, was first Machen's student at Princeton before following him to Philadelphia and graduating with the first class at Westminster. Machen delivered the pastoral charge for Ockenga's installation at Point Breeze Presbyterian Church in Pittsburgh. Among other things, Machen admonished the young pastor to keep central a deep engagement of the biblical text and to throw his net rather widely regarding the other disciplines:

> The whole world is your province as a preacher of the Gospel of Christ. Be interested in the teachings of science, in literature, in philosophy and art. Do not be content with a superficial study of the Holy Book, but be a scribe who has become a disciple of the Kingdom of God, who brings forth out of His treasure things new and old. Do not be content merely with a chance acquaintance with that Book, but seek to study it in light of the grand, exegetical tradition of the Christian Church. . . . As you study this book, new glories will be revealed and you will see that against it, all this world has to offer, with all its pleasures and all its turmoil and noise, is as nothing.

A well-trained clergy, Machen first learned in the tradition of Old Princeton and then endeavored to cultivate at Westminster, is the church's best defense and offense. Perhaps that best summarizes his philosophy of seminary education.

Efficient Education

Machen's thoughts and writings on education were not limited to the sphere of theology. In February of 1926, Machen testified in hearings before a joint session of committees of the House of Representatives and of the Senate of the United States concerning the Department of Education that was proposed to replace the existing bureau of education. That bureau did not enjoy a cabinet post and did not have the budget or powers of a department-level bureaucracy, and if Machen had his preference, it would stay that way. In keeping with his political libertarianism, as discussed in chapter 7, Machen opposed the department on principle, preferring individual liberty and states' rights over centralized federal control. Instead of American education under control of the Department of Education, Machen argued for the control of the individual states over public education and for private and parochial schools unencumbered by federal regulations. The formal statement he read into the congressional record came largely from an address he had delivered in January before the Sentinels of the Republic in Washington, D.C. He also had a lively exchange with senators and representatives who sat on the committees.

The new Department of Education would impose the standardization of education. While many cheered this, Machen thought otherwise, explaining that "standardization, it seems to me, destroys the personal character of human life." He further likened such standardization to the assembly lines at Henry Ford's motorcar company. But students, he argued, are not cars; they are individuals with idiosyncrasies—and he knew that teachers were, too. Instead, Machen argued for the preservation of the personal, free, and individual character of education.

He also foresaw that the new department would create a web of bureaucracy with large wheels, grinding slowly. Of course, that was the opposite argument advanced by proponents of the new department, who saw it as justified on the grounds of its efficiency. Machen used his penchant for humor in refuting this argument by telling the story of a tramp who made it to the third floor of a department store before finding himself systematically kicked down the floors until he landed on the sidewalk. Machen closed the story by relaying, "He landed on his back, and got up and said in a tone of admiration, 'My! What a system.' " Even if the new department were efficient, which Machen doubted, its efficiency would simply be an enslavement, "the worst kind of slavery that could be devised—a slavery in the sphere of the mind."

In addition to objecting to the Department of Education on the matter of principle, he also objected on the basis of what such movements were doing to the nature and process of education. To Machen, the trend was toward a more pragmatic view of education that served utilitarian purposes of making people better citizens and preparing them for their life's work. In fact, Machen once spoke of such an education driven by pragmatic concerns as "one of the great evils of the day." The emphasis on things practical reflected a truncated view of learning and of the role of education for both minister and citizen alike. W. E. B. DuBois shared similar sentiments, though in an entirely different context. Writing just after the turn of the twentieth century, DuBois argued that education is not simply job or even life training; it has to do with cultivating one's character and with gaining an exposure to and appreciation of the grand heritage, in the case of Americans, of Western culture, saying in his well-known words, "I sit with Shakespeare and he winces not." Though DuBois could appreciate the contribution of the "industrial school," he knew that education entailed far more. DuBois even resonated with Machen's insistence on individual liberty as he asserted, "Out of the worship of the mass, must persist and evolve that higher individualism which the centres of culture protect; there must come a loftier respect for the sovereign human soul that seeks a freedom for expansion and self-development."

As Darryl Hart has noted, Machen was not just a theological conservative; he was also an educational conservative. On the cusp of the transformation of education to simply professional preparation, Machen intoned that institutions of higher learning are obligated "to tell the student that there is no royal road to learning, that short-cuts lead to disaster, and that underneath all true research lies a broad foundation of general culture." He stressed content, when those around him cried "method." Yet the peculiar thing is that Machen was much loved by his students, considered an excellent communicator who kept their attention even when the subject happened to be Greek verb paradigms, and regarded as a highly successful faculty member at Princeton, even during the years of the controversy. "You never came late to a Machen class," one of his former students said. "He was a teacher who not only knew his subject, but one who could teach it well."

Conclusion

John Adams once advised his young son and the future President, "You will never be alone with a poet in your pocket"—advice taken by John Quincy Adams, known to read daily from the great poets. This advice was also taken by Machen's father, and even by Machen himself. In fact, as Machen learned the practice from his father, his father had learned it from his. The typical day of Lewis H. Machen, Machen's paternal grandfather, had time for the office, time for exercise—mostly gardening—time for family, and time in both morning and evening for reading the Bible. He also set aside up to an hour and a half a day for reading poetry—the English poets, to be sure, but also the French and German poets and the ancient Romans and Greeks, always in the original languages. His son and Machen's father, Arthur Webster Machen, followed in his footsteps.

In addition to being chief clerk of the United States Senate, Arthur's father owned a farm in Virginia. When he was in Washington while Congress was in session, the farm had to be run by hired hands and by his sons. Arthur would often write to his father to update him on activities. On one occasion he was driving a herd of a hundred steers to Georgetown. He took with him a volume of Horace, writing to his father of the journey, "Meantime time glides quickly. Fortunately, I carry a resource in my pocket. Yesterday when stopping for a few moments to give my steers a breath of fresh air under the shade of some oaks, I opened the volume at random and struck upon some most admirable directions as to diet." Arthur eventually moved from farming to law, but he never gave up his love of Horace or of being a lifelong learner. And he did quite well in passing on the same passion to his son. Machen often carried one of the volumes of the Loeb Classical Library with him, handy enough to fit in his coat pocket.

But it would be a mistake to see Machen as the bookworm or the stodgy academic. This is the same Machen who doodled notes while a student in seminary, and the same Machen who skipped Hebrew class to catch a Princeton football game. Henry W. Coray, one of Machen's students at Princeton and Westminster, recalled that Machen often said, "Boys, there are two things wrong with this institution: you're not working hard enough and you're not having enough fun." "You can't be a good theologian," another oft-repeated admonition began, "unless you're a good stunter." These help us see the full picture of Machen when we look upon the portrait of the figure clad in his academic regalia and about his scholarly business. We see that just as Machen learned from Old Princeton that one can have both piety and intellect together, religious devotion and intellectual rigor fused into one, so too he learned that one can be a good scholar and a good stunter.

A Note on the Sources

For a number of Machen's significant essays on Christian scholarship, theological education, and the Princeton Seminary controversy, including "The Importance of Christian Scholarship" and his opening address at Westminster, see J. Gresham Machen, *Selected Shorter Writings*, edited by D. G. Hart (2004). For a collection of Machen's writings on education, including his testimony before Congress, see J. Gresham Machen, *Education, Christianity and the State*, edited by John Robbins (1995). For the references to Machen's grandfather and father, see Arthur W. Machen, *Letters of Arthur W. Machen with Biographical Sketch* (1917). The references to W. E. B. DuBois are from his *The Souls of Black Folk* (1903). For vignettes of Machen as student, teacher, and scholar, see Henry W. Coray, *J. Gresham Machen: A Silhouette* (1981). See also D. G. Hart, *Defending the Faith* (1994), 105–6. For a thorough study of Princeton Theological Seminary, see David Calhoun's two-volume *Princeton Seminary* (1994, 1996). For a study of the broader context of American higher education, see George M. Marsden, *The Soul of the American University: From Protestant Establishment to Established Nonbelief* (1994).

PART 4

MACHEN AS CHURCHMAN: WRITINGS ON THE CHURCH AND SERMONS

Machen reluctantly became ordained. At one point in his life, he had ruled out the ministry altogether. But that was only at one time. As the years progressed, the role of churchman became a crucial one for J. Gresham Machen. Attending his first General Assembly as a commissioner in 1920, he became heavily engaged in the church throughout the latter years of his life. While most think of him as a scholar first, his legacy includes both a mission and a denomination, as well as a host of writings on the nature and purpose of the church. In these final chapters we will explore this significant aspect of his legacy. Chapter 10 begins with Machen's troubles with his own denomination, stemming from his challenge to the Presbyterian Church in the U.S.A.'s Board of Foreign Missions. Here we see Machen at work organizing not only a new mission, but also a new denomination after he is kicked out of his old one. The final two chapters treat a considerable part of his literary legacy by examining a few of his many sermons. As with his other writings, these texts reflect his clarity of thought and expression and his ability to speak to both his own and future generations.

10

A Doctrinal Church: Machen, Missions, and the Church

We are a doctrinal church.

Francis Landey Patton,
May 23, 1895

The suspension of Dr. Machen from the Ministry of our
Church will do him no injury; it will only increase his
influence and add to the far-flung echo of his voice.

Clarence E. N. Macartney, June 7, 1936

In 1895, the Presbyterian Church in the U.S.A. had reason to celebrate. A quarter of a century earlier had marked the reunion of the Old and New School Presbyterian Churches. Twenty-five years and still united—for Presbyterians, that was quite a reason to celebrate. The General Assembly ordered an anniversary service to be held at the First and Third Presbyterian Churches in Pittsburgh, inviting, among others, Francis Landey Patton, then president of Princeton University and soon-to-be friend and mentor of J. Gresham Machen, to speak. Patton spoke of the importance of doctrine to the Presbyterian Church. It was doctrine that had caused the split between Old School and New School Presbyterians, he noted, and it was doctrine that had led to the reunion. "We are," he proclaimed, "a doctrinal church." Unity prevailed, not in spite of but because of doctrine. Within another generation, that would change.

Machen's troubles with the Presbyterian Church began brewing in the early 1920s. He was first appointed to attend the General Assembly in 1920. The pressing issue then was the Plan of Unity, a call to increasingly ecumenical activities that Machen, among others, saw as leading to a downplaying of doctrine and Presbyterian distinctives. Then came Harry Emerson Fosdick, the Auburn Affirmation, and the politics and problems at Princeton. As we saw in earlier chapters, during this decade one wave of conflict rolled out upon another. Machen weathered them all—even his departure from Princeton and his establishment of Westminster. But the events of the early 1930s tipped the balance. Machen found himself stripped of his ministerial credentials, a minister without a church. This chapter looks beyond the events to explore some of Machen's writings on the controversy. Looking first at his statement on missions, we next explore his statement to the New Brunswick Presbytery. In the course of all the church politics, Machen sets forth in these documents what he sees as the essence of the church's task. Finally, we will examine some other texts rounding out Machen's understanding of the church.

It is curious to see again, as we have been seeing regularly with Machen, the way in which his response to modernism and liberalism differed from that of his conservative and fundamentalist cohorts. He once wrote of his ambivalence toward being called a fundamentalist, explaining, "There is, indeed, no inherent objection to the term; and if the disjunction is between 'Fundamentalism' and 'Modernism,' then I am willing to call myself a Fundamentalist of the most pronounced type." But Machen's preference lay elsewhere. He continued, noting his "warmest sympathy with other evangelical churches," adding, "But . . . I think I can best serve my fellow-Christians—even those who belong to ecclesiastical bodies different from my own—by continuing to be identified, very specifically, with the Presbyterian Church." Even after the Presbyterian Church no longer wished to have Machen identified with it, he never lost sight of his Presbyterian identity and commitments. When Machen was kicked out of the front door of the church, using the words of Pearl S. Buck, he, with others, started another one. And to be sure, "Presbyterian" was in the name.

The Importance of Missions

It may be recalled from chapter 3 that a report entitled *Re-Thinking Missions* from 1932 sparked a great controversy felt throughout American Christianity and especially acutely in the Presbyterian Church. Machen found it to be nothing short of abominable, and the reluctance of the Board of Foreign Missions of the church to speak out against it just about as abhorrent. That, coupled with the presence of Pearl S. Buck among the numbers of missionaries under the auspices of the board, in addition to other missionaries who were signers of the Auburn Affirmation and who outrightly denied such doctrines as the virgin birth, gave pause to Machen. He responded by drafting an overture to be presented to the New Brunswick Presbytery that, if it passed there, would then make it on the docket for the denomination's General Assembly in 1933. Machen did not do so with reckless abandon, neither did he relish the occasion. In fact, as he put it, his knowledge of the situation and his perceived task in responding to it fell upon him as a wearisome burden. "I should be far happier," he wrote in the foreword to his overture, "if I did not know certain things about the Board of Foreign Missions of the Presbyterian Church in the U.S.A.; but I do know those things, and the knowledge of them places upon me a duty which I cannot evade."

Machen's overture was rather straightforward. Making four points, he called upon the board to tighten the reins, electing only theological conservatives to the board and ensuring that missionaries believed in such central truths as the virgin birth and atoning death of Christ. He also wanted the denomination to take only those missionaries who evidenced "an unswerving faithfulness in the proclamation of the gospel as it is contained in the Word of God." This latter point grew out of the spirit and the letter of *Re-Thinking Missions* and the growing tolerance and pluralism in the atmosphere of the church. Machen countered, writing elsewhere in his essay "The Responsibility of the Church in Our New Age," by stressing that the church is to be "radically intolerant." This spirit of intolerance stretches back to the era of the beginning of the church and the time of the apostles. As Machen observes, "That was an age of synchronism and tolerance in religion." In response to that spirit of the age, as Machen notes, "[the Christian church] demanded a completely exclusive devotion. A man . . . could not accept the salvation offered by Christ and at the same time admit that for other people there might be some other way of salvation; he could not agree to refrain from proselytizing among men of other faiths, but came forward, no matter what it might cost, with a universal appeal." That response marked the "primitive church," and Machen viewed it as the only response of the modern church as well. But his was not the exclusive opinion of the Presbyterian Church in the U.S.A., nor of all the members of the mission board or of all the missionaries. Machen's overture continues for just over one hundred pages, carefully documenting the errors of the board and the encroachment of pluralism on the mission field.

It is important to see this conflict with the Board of Foreign Missions as the root of Machen's ouster from the church. First, it shows that Machen's quibble, far from being on the periphery, stemmed from the very heart of the gospel and the church's commitment to it. Often accused of being cantankerous and curmudgeonly, Machen contended with the church for what he knew was worth fighting for. He was not simply an out-of-step personality; he was contending for the faith. Further, this disagreement was not a matter of mere church politics. The issue was the preaching of either the gospel of Christ as given in Scripture or another message altogether. Quite literally, lives were at stake. The cause of disagreement is also important to see because the way in which this conflict unfolded led directly to the dismissal. Machen's overture never reached the floor of the General Assembly because of its defeat at the New Brunswick Presbytery. It would not have mattered even if it had. Similar overtures, passing through more conservative presbyteries, did make it to the floor of the General Assembly, only to go nowhere. Now Machen faced a dilemma. He thought that he could no longer in good conscience support the mission agency of his denomination, financially or otherwise. Consequently, he, with a small band of others, founded the Independent Board of Presbyterian Foreign Missions.

The new board began in earnest in 1933, enlisting the services of Charles Woodbridge, a missionary in then French Cameroon, to serve as general secretary. Funds were collected, with Machen contributing a great deal. By 1934 the first missionaries, Henry Coray (originally Machen's student at Princeton and then at Westminster who also wrote a biography of Machen) and his wife, arrived in China to begin their work. And just as quickly, denominational leaders began attacking the board as unconstitutional. By the 1934 General Assembly, the groundwork had been laid to bring those associated with the new Independent Board under discipline.

Machen first responded to the directive of the General Assembly to cease his activity with the Independent Board by writing a lengthy "Statement" to the New Brunswick Presbytery. In the one hundred or so pages of his statement, Machen makes the case that the new board came about only as a last resort, and only after his attempts, as well as those of others, to have the denomination address the crisis within its own mission board. He then sets forth his case as to "Why I cannot obey the order of the General Assembly." Chief among his arguments stands his reason that "obedience . . . would involve support of a propaganda that is contrary to the gospel of Christ." Machen's allegiance to the gospel was paramount. Consequently, he viewed following the General Assembly's order as involving "the substitution of a human authority for the authority of the Word of God." The Independent Board was, in Machen's view, recalcitrant and, having been set on such a course, could not be turned back.

Not all of Machen's contemporaries, even among his supporters, saw it quite that way. There were those, such as Clarence Macartney and Samuel Craig, who thought that Machen's work in establishing the Independent Board was too divisive, that it would precipitate a split, that it effectively cut off all hopes of reform of the church, and finally, that it would endanger the valuable work just begun at Westminster Theological Seminary in filling the denomination with solid ministers. In one sense they were right. The action left Machen first marginalized and then cut off from his de-

10.1. Machen often reworked his material, as his typewritten manuscript page of "What the Church Stands For" is transformed to "Safeguarding the Church."

nomination, losing any opportunity to reform from within. Machen, however, had already faced his share of troubles with the church, and probably thought taking his stand more valuable than continuing to hold out hope for reform.

As he had written in his article published in Craig's *Christianity Today* in 1931, titled "The Truth about the Presbyterian Church," signers of the Auburn Affirmation were ubiquitously present in the denomination, serving not only on the mission board, but also on other key committees and boards and as editors of the denominational newspapers. Modernism was choking the assembly, with the result that "the entire machinery of the church is dominated by a Modernist-indifferentist tendency which is in striking contradiction both to the Bible and the church's Confession of Faith." Even then, Machen hoped to overcome the tide. But that was in 1931. By 1933, he did more than simply write against the church; he directly challenged it through the new mission board. The result was a protracted time of debate and the toilsome burden of a church trial for Machen and his compatriots. In the end, Machen lost and was suspended from his ministry in the Presbyterian Church in the U.S.A.

Clarence Macartney, speaking shortly after Machen's suspension was formally and finally announced, defended his friend and former Princeton classmate. Although he would not go along with Machen in his decision to found the new mission board, an action causing a grievous rift in their relationship, Macartney never lost his respect for Machen's character and admiration of his courage. Macartney, perhaps desirous of healing the rift, expressed, "I am glad in this public way to testify my affection for him, my confidence in the purity of his character and the sincerity of his motives." He then declared, "The suspension of Dr. Machen from the Ministry of our Church will do him no injury; it will only increase his influence and add to the far-flung echo of his voice. He is suspended from the Ministry of the Presbyterian Church of the United States of America but few if any will think of him as suspended from the Ministry of our Lord Jesus Christ." Macartney was right: in the same month in which he spoke these words, Machen was already at work organizing a new church.

A Thirst for the Word: The Nature and Mission of the Church

As early as 1924, Machen had already clearly seen the essence of the conflict within the church, which he expressed in the pages of *The Presbyterian:* "The Presbyterian Church in the United States of America has apparently come to the parting of the ways. It may stand for Christ, or it may stand against him; but it can hardly halt between the two opinions." Despite Machen's fair warning, the church tried to hover in the middle as best it could. Machen himself hoped for, and he worked toward, a resolution, but not for the one that came. In his solution, the liberal contingent would have to leave the church. Let the liberals believe as they will, Machen averred, reflective of his commitment to individual liberty and his utter aversion to compulsion. He just kindly asked them to no longer occupy the Presbyterian Church. As Machen wrote in the closing paragraphs of his brief autobiographical sketch, "Christianity in Conflict," first published in 1932, "If [a minister] adopts some position other than that of the Presbyterian Church, let him have full liberty to become a minister in some other body." But, of course, this was not the way it turned out. Instead, Machen found himself out the door. The rejection, however, paved the way for Machen to establish one more institution, the Presbyterian Church of America, renamed the Orthodox Presbyterian Church.

Machen's involvement in the new church would be brief, cut off by his untimely death on January 1, 1937. But in the short six months or so that Machen could give to the church, he endeavored to infuse it with as much of his imprint as he could. Machen might very well have been thinking about the new church since the early 1920s and his last conversation with B. B. Warfield, in which Princeton's elder statesman reminded the younger that "you can't split rotten wood"—which Machen took as a prediction of a soon-coming new church. The summer of 1936 readily afforded him the opportunity to put whatever thoughts and theories he had about the church into action. At bottom, Machen longed for the same church that Patton had spoken of in 1895, a doctrinal one, a church founded on the message of the atoning death of Christ and one that would proclaim that message faithfully in the preaching of the Word and administering of the sacraments.

In fact, Machen had a bit more time than the mere summer months of 1936 to put the church together. Anticipating the rulings of the General Assembly, conservatives in the denomination earlier in 1935 drafted a "Covenant Union." The Covenant's express purpose, as set forth in the preamble, was "to defend the Presbyterian Church in the USA." Of course, the drafters of the Covenant Union, Machen among them, had quite a different vision from the denominational leaders at the time. Nevertheless, the preamble continued the explanation of the Covenant Union's purpose:

> To defend (1) the Word of God upon which the Constitution [of the church] is based, (2) the full, glorious system of revealed truth contained in the [Westminster] Confession of Faith and Catechisms, commonly called (to distinguish it from various forms of error) the "Reformed Faith", and (3) the truly Scriptural principles of Presbyterian Church government, guaranteeing the Christian's freedom from implicit obedience to any human councils and courts, recognizing instead, in the high Biblical sense, the authority of God.

The Covenant Union went on to express that those who signed it also pledged to make "every effort to bring about a reform of the existing church organization." Barring that, the signers also pledged "to perpetuate the True Presbyterian Church in the USA, regardless of cost." The cost was great, to be sure.

What the Covenant Union reveals is that Machen and his like-minded colleagues were intent on not simply a new church, but a new church committed to historic Presbyterianism. And Machen made sure that this would be the case in the new church. A lengthy quotation from his sermon before the Second General Assembly of the new church bears out this commitment:

> What a privilege to proclaim not some partial system of truth but the full, glorious system which God has revealed in his Word, and which is summarized in the wonderful [Westminster] Standards of our faith! What a privilege to get those hallowed instruments, in which that truth is summarized, down from the shelf and write them in patient instruction, by the blessing of the Holy Spirit, upon the tablets of our children's hearts! What a privilege to present our historic Standards in all their fullness in the pulpit and at the teacher's desk and in the Christian home! What a privilege to do that for the one reason that those Standards present, not a "man-made creed," but what God has told in His holy Word.

The commitment to the Westminster Standards of historic Presbyterianism, in Machen's view, reflected a commitment to the authority and centrality of God's Word. As he makes clear in *Christianity and Liberalism,* it is the Bible and the cross of Christ that define Christianity.

Martin Luther once wrote, "We can spare everything except the Word." And when the reformer thought about the marks of the true church, which he did often, the Word of God and the centrality of preaching it always topped the list. Machen, though a confirmed Presbyterian, could not agree with the founder of Lutheranism more. The emphasis on the Word of God not only shines through in Machen's public writings, but also overflows in his correspondence. One example among many concerns a letter he received from Walter Buchanan, a Presbyterian minister in New York City, in 1926. He was seeking Machen's advice on a matter in-

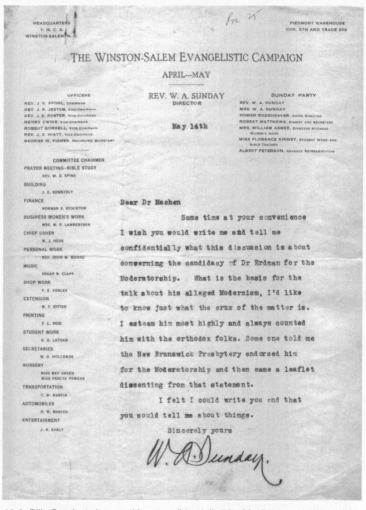

10.2. Billy Sunday's letter asking, "confidentially," for Machen's estimation of Charles Erdman for moderator of the 1925 General Assembly.

volving a union of two Presbyterian churches in Morristown, New Jersey. The union ensured that the theological conservatives would be among the minority in the new church. Unhappy with the merger, the minority broke and, as Buchanan relates in the letter to Machen, "[were] now worshipping in a town hall and [were] in need of hymn books." They were appealing to Buchanan's church to sell them hymnals.

Buchanan was not sure what to do, reflective of his sense that the minority should appeal to the General Assembly before breaking off and maybe even because of the paranoia caused by an ever-aggressive General Assembly. In any event, he sought Machen's advice. Machen knew the situation firsthand, having recently preached to the conservative group. He opted not to advise Buchanan on the sale of hymnals, but he did say this: "I preached for them in the Municipal Building Sunday before last, and I am going to preach for them again on the 28th. They have a thirst for the Word of God, which has come from a long absence of it in Morristown, and I find them a very repaying congregation to preach to." He added, "They are fine people, and they have a great longing for real worship of God on the basis of the gospel—a thing of which they are deprived in Morristown." Machen empathized with that group, knowing that there were likely many others in the denomination. Consequently, when he formed the Orthodox Presbyterian Church, he was sure to stress that above all it would preach the gospel. "What privilege," he told those assembled for the second General Assembly of the new church, "to proclaim [the message of the cross] to the souls of people who sit in nominally Christian churches and starve for lack of the bread of life!"

His commitment to the centrality of the Word of God also surfaces in a curious exchange of correspondence regarding an invitation to preach at Seal Harbor, Maine. During those summers that his family vacationed at Seal Harbor, Machen preached on occasion at the little Seal Harbor Union Church to a congregation of mostly fellow vacationers, including on many July and August Sundays the likes of John D. Rockefeller. William Adams Brown, a professor at Union Theological Seminary who was in charge of filling the pulpit in the summer of 1924, wrote to Machen, inviting him once again to take a few Sundays. He added, "It is not necessary to remind you . . . that it is possible for those of widely different intellectual beliefs about Christianity to meet in common worship." Machen accepted, but he could not resist the urge to say a thing or two concerning Brown's reminder in the acceptance letter. He expressed that he was not in sympathy with Brown's views. To Machen, there could be true worship and fellowship only with those committed to a doctrinal center of intellectual beliefs. A social club Machen was not interested in. To him, the true church was found gathered only around the Word—precisely what the world around it needs. As Machen told the Second General Assembly, "What a wonderful open door God has placed before the church of today. A Pagan world, weary and sick, often distrusting its own modern gods. A saving gospel strangely entrusted to us unworthy messengers. A Divine book of unused resources of glory and power. Ah, what a marvelous opportunity, my brethren!"

Machen viewed this commitment to the Word as central not only to the church's preaching, but also to its fellowship and outreach. In *Christianity and Liberalism,* he spoke of the many who were "troubled by grave doubts," adding, "For great hosts of such troubled souls the Church offers bountifully its fellowship and its aid; it would be a crime to cast them out. There are many men of little faith in our troublous times. . . . God grant that they may obtain comfort and help through the ministrations of the Church!" The church, in Machen's estimation, is the sole place where those seeking "refuge from the strife" and weary from the turmoil of the world "unite at the foot of the cross." One senses the incredible wave of joy and relief when Machen, upon the founding of the new church, exclaimed, "We recovered, at last, true Christian fellowship. What a joyous moment it was!" That burst of emotion seems to communicate that somehow all the struggles that Machen faced in his battles over the church's mission board and with its leadership, not to mention the countless details and demands of the new denomination, were well worthwhile.

Conclusion

Machen's legacy involves not only his writings, but also the institutions that he founded. In Westminster Seminary, his commitment to scholarship and a well-trained clergy—"specialists in the Bible"—displays itself. And in the Orthodox Presbyterian Church (and, many would argue, also in the Presbyterian Church in America and other denominations), his commitment to the church comes to the fore as well. Machen was a scholar among scholars, while also a churchman, pulling off that rare but delightful blend. In his role as churchman, he viewed his task as no different from that of his work as scholar: the proclamation and defense of the gospel of Christ.

And when the church maintains its sacred trust in preaching the gospel, it does not lose; it wins—despite all appearances to the contrary. As Machen wrote in *Christianity and Liberalism*, "God has not deserted His Church; He has brought her through even darker hours than those which try our courage now, yet the darkest hour has always come before the dawn. . . . But meanwhile our souls are tried. We can only try to do our duty in humility and in sole reliance upon the Saviour who bought us with His blood." That was in 1923. The dark hours continued to come, and the trying of souls wore on. At the 1936 General Assembly, Machen was vastly in the minority. A mere handful of ministers and elders joined him in breaking ranks from the large and prominent Presbyterian Church in the U.S.A. He, and they, suffered a humiliating defeat at the hands of the General Assembly, playing the classic role of David against Goliath, only on this occasion Goliath walked off the battlefield. The new denomination numbered approximately five thousand against the two million strong of the Presbyterian Church in the U.S.A. Yet as Robert Churchill, who as a young man was with the new church from 1936 on, reminisced, "Though [the Orthodox Presbyterian Church's] numbers may be relatively small, the church stands for something quite big." Machen knew that just as the world's plaudits were not the true measure, neither were the judgments of a church that had deserted its sacred trust. He took comfort in the rightness of the new denomination's cause, not the strength of its numbers.

Accordingly, as moderator of the Second General Assembly, he charged the young church in his sermon entitled "Constraining Love" that because of Christ's love, "we shall be constrained, for example, not to weaken in the stand which we have for the sake of Christ. How many movements have begun bravely like this one, and then have been deceived by Satan—have been deceived by Satan into belittling controversy, condoning sin and error, seeking favor from the world or from a worldly church." Machen knew that something far greater than the machinations of the General Assembly was ultimately at work. He also knew that, above all, the church was faithful in its work only when it proclaimed the gospel of Christ. Appropriately, Machen closed his autobiographical reflections expressing that commitment:

> Our real confidence rests not in the signs of the times, but in the great and precious promises of God. Contrast the glories of God's Word with the weak and beggarly elements of this mechanistic age, contrast the liberty of the sons of God with the ever-increasing slavery into which mankind is falling in our time, and I think we shall come to see with a new clearness, despite the opposition of the world, that we have no reason to be ashamed of the gospel of Christ.

A Note on the Sources

Two significant texts by Machen dealing with the details of his controversy over the Board of Foreign Missions are *Modernism and the Board of Foreign Missions of the Presbyterian Church in the U.S.A.*, privately printed by Machen in 1933, and his *Statement to the Special Committee of the Presbytery of New Brunswick,* also privately printed by Machen in 1934. A selection of the latter, as well as other pertinent essays, may be found in J. Gresham Machen, *Selected Shorter Writings,* edited by D. G. Hart (2004). See Machen's chapter on the church in *Christianity and Liberalism* (1923), 157–80. His sermon "Constraining Love" is reprinted in William S. Barker and Samuel T. Logan Jr., *Sermons That Shaped America* (2003), 344–61. For discussions on Machen, the missions controversy, and the church, see Robert K. Churchill, *Lest We Forget* (1986); Henry W. Coray, *J. Gresham Machen* (1981), 75–128; D. G. Hart, *Defending the Faith* (1994), 133–59; Edwin H. Rian, *The Presbyterian Conflict* (1940); Ned B. Stonehouse, *J. Gresham Machen* (1987), 469–508; and Paul Woolley, *The Significance of Machen Today* (1977), 35–43. Additionally, a number of helpful essays on Machen and the

Orthodox Presbyterian Church may be found in Charles G. Dennison, *History for a Pilgrim People*, edited by Danny O. Olinger and David K. Thompson (2002), and *Pressing Toward the Mark*, edited by Charles G. Dennison and Richard C. Gamble (1986).

11

"THE GOOD FIGHT OF FAITH": A SERMON PREACHED IN MILLER CHAPEL, PRINCETON THEOLOGICAL SEMINARY, MARCH 10, 1929

> *I hope above all that, wherever you are and however*
> *your preaching may be received, you may be true*
> *witnesses for the Lord Jesus Christ.*
>
> J. Gresham Machen, *"The Good Fight of Faith"*

Faculty often do more than teach. And for those on the faculty of Princeton Theological Seminary, part of their extra responsibilities entailed preaching in Miller Chapel, a building essentially the same now as it was in Machen's day. On one such occasion, he preached a sermon just under three weeks before he was to board the steamer for France to commence his fourteen-month service with the YMCA in the Great War. Certainly, it would be quite understandable if Machen were not in top form. He had been quite busy making arrangements to leave, and a cloud of anxiety hovered overhead. Yet it was a most profound moment. Rebekah Purves Armstrong, the wife of his trusted friend and mentor William Park Armstrong ("Army"), captured the moment in a letter to Machen's mother:

> I wish you could have been with us on Sunday and heard him preach in the Chapel. It was an impressive service, the Chapel was filled and Gresham's power as a preacher was never more evident, but what impressed me especially was the earnestness and beauty of his prayers. The congregation was moved in a way I have seldom seen. Such gifts as his will surely be used by God to carry conviction and healing to men in trouble.

Machen preached often, and not just in Miller Chapel. From the 1920s on, rarely did a Sunday go by without finding Machen in a pulpit somewhere, and that somewhere often took him quite far from home. At times, as described in his letters, he chafed under the fatigue and other demands of his itinerant preaching. Typically, those moments passed quickly, however, as he found himself rejuvenated by the ministry of preaching the Word. In other words, he enjoyed preaching and did it quite often. Part of Machen's literary legacy includes those sermons. They do not constitute a great mass, partly because his itinerant schedule allowed him to repreach sermons, some of them again and again and again. A humorous letter during his time in Paris immediately after the armistice reveals his dilemma in being invited to give seven sermons, when he had only "six in the barrel." That was in 1918. Through the 1920s, of course, he added a great many more to his sermon barrel.

His longest stint as a preacher came when he served as stated supply for the First Presbyterian Church in Princeton from 1923 to 1924. A number of those sermons have

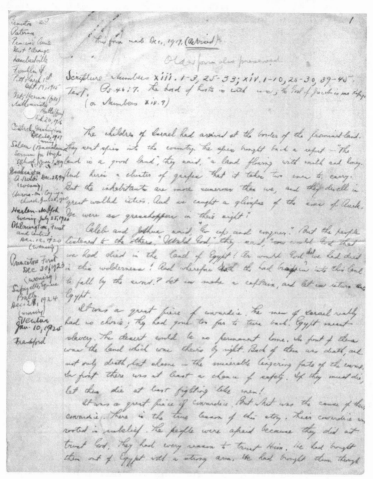

11.1. A handwritten sermon manuscript. In the left column, Machen recorded the numerous times he preached the sermon.

been reprinted in a collection entitled *God Transcendent*, edited by Ned Stonehouse and published posthumously. Otherwise, his sermons were quite occasional, which is helpful to keep in mind when looking at his sermon corpus. We do not have a series of sermons by Machen in which he preaches through a book of the Bible, for instance. But what we do find are a number of sermons that, like the one preached in Miller Chapel in 1918, came with great power, with conviction, and with healing. This is not due to Machen's eloquence, although he could be quite literary. Rather, it is due to his conviction that preaching is simply allowing the Word of God to shine through. As testament to his abilities in the pulpit, one of his sermons has recently been reprinted, in *American Sermons: The Pilgrims to Martin Luther King Jr.,* published by The Library of America (1999); and one of his sermons, also preached at Miller Chapel, found its way into *Best Sermons, 1926,* published by Harcourt, Brace, and Co.

One of his earliest sermons, a requirement for his senior preaching class while a student at Princeton, treats 2 Timothy 3:16, extolling the necessity of Scripture as "the only infallible rule of faith and practice." His sermons were also attended by conviction and healing because of his consistent reference to the cross and to the gospel of Christ. One has to try hard not to notice the cross somewhere lifted up for his hearers to see. This chapter looks at this aspect of Machen's legacy by exploring one sermon in particular, "The Good Fight of Faith," another sermon preached in Miller Chapel on an auspicious occasion, the eve before his departure from his beloved institution. Before discussing that sermon, however, a slight detour into Machen's thoughts on preaching might further help to set the stage to understand both his sermons and his legacy as a pastor.

On Preaching

Most of the time, Machen preached from a full manuscript. That's not to suggest that he always read his sermons or that he was tied to the manuscript. There were also times when he preached from an outline. One such time, again speaking to students at Princeton Seminary in Miller Chapel,

Machen gave a "Chapel Talk" on the subject of preaching. It is a fascinating manuscript, simply a single-page outline. Yet in all its terseness it speaks volumes about Machen's take on preaching. He looks at six elements of a sermon and the nature of preaching. First, he mentions the sermon's introduction. He notes, even rhyming perhaps to help students remember his point, that the introduction should be geared to arousing interest, that it should take into account "the point of view of the man in the pew." This immediately leads him to offer some "Practical Hints," the first of which is "Not over 30 minutes"—Machen was helping the young seminarians not to become too verbose. His second practical hint concerns style. Preachers should, he observes, "avoid artificiality," a point he further develops by encouraging them to watch their "tone," and, reflective of his anti-romantic tendencies, to avoid "hackneyed and sentimental illustrations."

His next four points concern more theoretical issues, looking first at exegesis and preaching. Under this head, he encouraged the future pastors to "go deeper" in the biblical text by using "critical commentaries [that will] bring [you] into contact with [the] Bible itself." He then adds, "[The] Bible is the only way to avoid monotony and [the] commonplace because of [the] varied hist[orical] forms of its teaching." When Machen and the others involved in establishing Westminster Theological Seminary looked for a motto, they landed on "Preach the whole counsel of God." And that principle was what Machen had in mind here. Not to be missed is the way in which Machen begins with the Bible when he discusses the content of the message. He also, however, has a close eye on bringing the Bible to bear upon the contemporary reader.

Consequently, his next point concerns "Modern Thought and Preaching." "Belief against [the Bible and the] opposition is powerful," he notes, warning that not all are receptive to the Word of God, especially with the onset of modernism and liberalism. He then asks how the seminarians would respond to the present situation: "Are you going to drift with [the] current and say (a) not theol[ogy] but life or (b) not creed, but service? Or are you going to rediscover the gospel?" Even in 1914, Machen was hammering the theme that would come to full fruition in his classic book from 1923, *Christianity and Liberalism,* that Christianity is first a doctrine. Further, even in 1914, he sensed the forces at work to reduce Christianity to sentimental and experiential expression. And in light of those pressures, he called this next generation of pastors to stand their ground.

His final two points concern what goes into the person preaching more than what goes into the sermon. Beginning with "Meditation and Preaching," he notes rather cryptically, "Mary and Martha. We need to *receive* from Jesus before we give to Him." Drawing on the familiar story of Mary and Martha, Machen makes the point that preaching stems from a relationship that one has with Christ. This naturally flows into Machen's last point concerning "Christ and Preaching." Again, he merely writes, "The power of Christ for the modern world." His point, however, can be by no means mistaken. He echoes Paul's battle cry to preach "Christ and him crucified," from 1 Corinthians 2:1–2. Not only did Machen speak of these virtues of preaching to his students at Princeton, he also frequently spoke of them at Westminster Seminary. In a powerful way he once challenged a graduating class of future ministers from the seminary in Philadelphia, reminding them that they were "called to deal with the unseen things," continuing:

> You are stewards of the mysteries of God. You alone can lead men, by the proclamation of God's word, out of the crash and jazz and noise and rattle and smoke of this weary age

into the green pastures and beside still waters; you alone, as ministers of reconciliation, can give what the world with all its boasting and pride can never give—the infinite sweetness of the communion of the redeemed soul with the living God.

The preaching of the gospel, according to Machen, is attended by great power, the power to convict and to heal. Not all of Machen's contemporaries agreed. Many of them were jettisoning the gospel and neglecting, as Machen says at one point, to offer the bread of life to a starving generation. To them the gospel had become irrelevant, an outdated and mythological concept no longer holding sway over the modern mind. Machen knew otherwise. One of the earliest books on the nature of preaching, the Puritan William Perkins's *The Art of Prophesying*, noted that because "the Word of God is God's wisdom from heaven revealing the truth," it has "power to penetrate into the spirit of man." That was true for the Israelites, the first-century Greeks and Romans, and the English Puritans of the sixteenth century. It was no less true for modern culture in the twentieth century—or, for that matter, for postmodern culture in the twenty-first. Perhaps that is why Machen's sermons continue to convict and to heal. To be sure, he references people and events that contemporary readers may not directly connect with, such as World War I, the Depression, and Lindbergh's historic flight over the Atlantic Ocean. His preaching of Christ and him crucified, however, still has much to teach us today. This is readily clear in his sermon "The Good Fight of Faith."

Last Words at Princeton

In June 1929, Machen tendered his resignation to the board of Princeton Theological Seminary, marking the end of a long and fruitful and, for both Machen and his students, most remarkable time. He could no longer support the seminary's board, which as a result of the reorganization now numbered among its ranks two signers of the Auburn Affirmation and, perhaps even worse in Machen's estimation, a remaining body of "indifferentists," those who would not speak protest, even against the change. It was a sad moment for Machen. He had come to love Princeton, embraced its long and rich tradition, and enjoyed the camaraderie with colleagues and students—he also became quite fond of and spoiled by being within a stone's throw of its indispensable "large library." His departure captured the headlines of *The New York Times.* As he spelled out in frequent interviews with *The Times,* he could no longer stay at Princeton because that would signal tacit approval of the change, betraying "the evangelical people in the church." Machen left, mourning the loss of Old Princeton.

He left, then, essentially on principle, a principle that, he would contend, was well worth fighting for. The principle was a commitment to the authority of the Word of God and the centrality of the gospel of Christ, unmixed, unadulterated, and undiluted. For some time, amounting to decades, this had been his message, preached wherever his itinerary would take him, taught in his classes at Princeton, and expressed in the pages of his books, articles, and interviews. One of the most succinct expressions of this principle comes, rather curiously, in his last sermon addressed to the students at Princeton Theological Seminary in Miller Chapel on March 10, 1929, "The Good Fight of Faith." He knew that things at the seminary would probably go the same way of things in the denomination, but in the spring of 1929, and even through the month of May and the General Assembly of that year, he held out hope that the reorganization would not go through and "the light of old Princeton," which so cogently testified to that central principle, would not go out.

Machen expressed this hope in his speech as a commissioner to the 1929 General Assembly meeting in St. Paul, Minnesota. He admits that Princeton may very well be out of step with modern sensibilities in its commitment to "proclaiming an unpopular gospel, which runs counter to the whole current of the age." But he also adds, "Yet it is a gospel of which we are not ashamed." He then notes the tendency, however, for institutions to drift and depart from former commitments and traditions. Consequently, he concedes, that departure appears to be the case with Princeton at the moment. Because of this urgency, he implores the General Assembly not to allow the reorganization to go through, which, in Machen's estimation, would "destroy the old Princeton." His message, however, went unheeded.

That was not the case on March 10, 1929. At that point in time, Machen was not sure how events would materialize. Consequently, his sermon comes not in a context of despair, but in the context of hope, not as a desperate last gasp, but as a rallying cry. In selecting his biblical text for the sermon, Machen strung together two passages from Paul: "And the peace of God, which passeth all understanding, shall keep your hearts and minds through Jesus Christ," Philippians 4:7, and a phrase taken from 1 Timothy 6:12, "Fight the good fight of faith." On the surface they seem to be rather divergent texts. Peace is extolled in one, fighting in the other. Yet Machen sees a fitting connection between these texts, which both come at the conclusion to Paul's letters to the Philippians and to his protégé Timothy, respectively.

Paul's Paradox

Machen begins his sermon "Fight the Good Fight of Faith" by looking at the life of Paul, "a great fighter." His fighting at times entailed physical hardship, stemming from his adventures. "Lindbergh, I suppose, got a thrill when he hopped off to Paris, and people are in search of thrills today; but if you wanted a really unbroken succession of thrills, I think you can hardly do better than try knocking around the Roman Empire of the first century with the Apostle Paul, engaged in the unpopular business of turning the world upside down." The chief battles that he fought, however, were the ones "fought against the enemies in his own camp." "Read [his] epistles with care," Machen observes, "and you see Paul always in conflict." And at the heart of all of that conflict stood "the doctrine of divine grace, the centre and core of the gospel that Paul preached." He fought, Machen contends, for the gospel. At times, it appeared as though it was a losing battle, but "just as he seems to be defeated, his greatest triumphs, by God's grace, are in store." And, he tells the Princetonians, the real company of Paul are those who also fight. He even personalizes the message, exclaiming, "God grant that you—students in this seminary—may be fighters, too!"

He acknowledges that they actually have their own "battles even now: you have to contend against sins gross and refined; you have to contend against the sins of slothfulness and inertia; you have, many of you, I know very well, a mighty battle on your hands against doubt and despair." He reminds them, however, that they should not be discouraged by such battles, for the Christian life is, in the words of the title from one of John Bunyan's books, a "Holy War." Mentioning Bunyan, Machen can't resist referring to *The Pilgrim's Progress*, in which the allegory of the pilgrimage of the Christian life presents battles and conflict. Beyond the spiritual battles with which the students contend, Machen warns them of coming battles "when you go forth as ministers in the church." The opposition will come from without, but also, Machen laments, within the church. So he expresses what they will face: "If you decide to stand for Christ, you will not have an easy life in the ministry"—a lesson that Machen learned personally. Standing for Christ, in that context, meant certain sacrifices. But he adds, "Certainly in making that sacrifice we do not complain; for we have something with which all that we have lost is not worthy to be compared."

Yet fighting for the faith is not easy. Further, it is not always easy, Machen admits, to fight from the right motives. Some fight merely for the sake of it. He observes, however: "This battle is a battle of love; and nothing ruins a man's service in it so much as a spirit of hate." Machen leads them to another motive, a motive that will be the source of courage to stand in the conflict. He finds the answer in Paul, explaining, "The answer is paradoxical; but it is very simple. Paul was a great fighter because he was at peace. He who said 'Fight the good fight of faith,' spoke also of 'the peace of God which passeth all understanding'; and in that peace the sinews of war were found." His "peace within" enabled him to fight against "enemies without." "No, there is no other way to be a good fighter. You cannot fight God's battles against God's enemies," he continues, "unless you are at peace with Him."

Before following through on the implications of this paradox, he raises the question of how one finds peace with God. It comes only, as he points out, through the cross, the center of the faith worth fighting for. In a memorable few lines, he demonstrates the power of the cross, even for hearts of stone:

> The cross remains foolishness to the world, men turn coldly away, and our preaching seems but vain. And then comes the wonder of wonders! The hour comes for some poor soul, even through the simplest and poorest preaching; there comes a flash of light into the soul, and all is as clear as day. "He loved me and gave himself for me," says the sinner at last, as he contemplates the Saviour upon the cross. The burden of sin falls from the back, and a soul enters into the peace of God.

That, for Machen, constitutes preaching Christ and him crucified and the only way to have peace with God. But the possession of such peace leads one not away from but rather into conflict. Machen, introducing yet another dimension to the paradox, puts it this way: "Those who have been at the foot of the cross will not be afraid to go forth under the banner of the cross to a holy war of love." In the course of the controversy over Harry Emerson Fosdick and at Princeton, as well as in the controversy to come in the 1930s over the mission board, Machen became quite aware of the slippery and deceitful use of language by the modernists and liberals and even the moderates. The words *peace* and *love* and *unity* were thrown about with little care toward defining those terms or filling them with any semblance of meaning from biblical teaching. They became easy words to stop honest disagreement and discussion. As Machen witnessed again and again, they also became easy ways to discredit and dismiss. Peace and love and unity, however, exist only when centered on the gospel. And, as Machen points out, the paradoxical nature of peace leads one into, not away from, battle.

In the day and age in which the sermon was preached, there was a "great battle now rag[ing] in the church." A significant aspect of that battle concerned the fact that not all agreed with the need for the type of preaching that Machen insisted on. Not all agreed with the authority of the Bible or with its teaching of the person of Christ and the necessity of his atoning death on the cross for salvation. Machen puts the question directly to his hearers as to which side they will follow in the raging conflict. He goes on to say that he has many hopes for the young seminarians, but that "I hope above all that, wherever you are and however your preaching may be received, you may be true witnesses for the Lord Jesus Christ." He adds, "I hope that there may never be any doubt where *you* stand, but that you always may stand squarely for Jesus Christ, as He is offered to us, not in the experiences of men, but in the blessed written Word of God."

Of course, he advises, "I do not mean that the great issue of the day must be polemically presented in every sermon that you preach. No doubt that would be exceedingly unwise." But "when the occasion does arise to take a stand," he implores them not to "shrink back." "God grant, instead," he continues, "that in all humility, but also in all boldness, in reliance upon God, you may fight the good fight of faith!" And so he closes, returning to the paradox one last time: "Peace is indeed yours, the peace of God which passeth all understanding. But that peace is given you, not that you may be onlookers or neutrals in love's battle, but that you may be good soldiers of Jesus Christ."

Conclusion

Machen's sermon "The Good Fight of Faith" was originally directed to seminary students poised at a crucial moment in the history of the church. It had, in other words, a definite audience and a definite context. Yet it would be mistaken not to see the sermon's broader application for those not attending seminary and for those not living in 1929. In Paul's day, as the sermon detailed, Paul had the task of contending for the faith. Machen and his colleagues and students had it in their day, and we have the same task in our day as well. Taking a stand for the gospel of Christ is not always easy, at times out of step with the currents of the age and at times causing one to be ostracized. All the while, however, it remains the responsibility of the church, which entails all Christians, to "fight the good fight of faith." Beyond the enemies without the church, and even the enemies within the church, however, stand our own selves, full of doubts and frailty and shortcomings and weakness. Machen acknowledged this to be true of himself, at one point confessing that he proclaims the gospel in great weakness, with echoes of Paul in 2 Corinthians 4:7, quite "conscious of [his] unworthiness to be entrusted with a treasure so great." Yet Machen quickly pointed out that the authority of the gospel does not derive from us, neither is it sourced in our wisdom or dependent on our eloquence. Rather, it comes clothed in the power of the Holy Spirit and issues from "the blessed pages of the Word of God." Even the enemy of our own self is not a sufficient reason for pacifism in the fight of the faith.

One final word of advice from Machen is in order: "Remember this at least—the things in which the world is now interested are the things that are seen." But "out of the crash and jazz and noise and rattle and smoke of this weary age" we have the privilege of pointing people to "the infinite sweetness of the communion of the redeemed soul with the living God." We have the message of peace.

A Note on the Sources

"The Good Fight of Faith" has been reprinted, along with other sermons, in *God Transcendent* (1982), 128–40. For a brief discussion of Machen's preaching, see Henry W. Coray, *J. Gresham Machen* (1981), 60–64. For Machen's last days at Princeton Seminary, see D. G. Hart, *Defending the Faith* (1994), 122–32, and Ned B. Stonehouse, *J. Gresham Machen* (1987), 430–45. For additional sermons and radio addresses of Machen, see his *The Christian Faith in the Modern World* (1936, reprinted 1965) and *The Christian View of Man* (1937, reprinted 1965).

12

THE CROSS OF CHRIST: SELECT SERMONS FROM DECEMBER 1936

To the sinner saved by grace how sweet a thing it is to contemplate the cross of Christ.

> J. Gresham Machen,
> "Christ Our Redeemer," December 6, 1936

I am so thankful for [the] active obedience of Christ. No hope without it.

> J. Gresham Machen,
> telegram to John Murray, January 1, 1937

Sometimes death comes so suddenly that it leaves no occasion for the recording of one's last words. This is unfortunate, for those last words often serve as a clear-eyed summation of the meaning of a life and as good a picture as any of the heart and soul of the one making the utterance. Machen's death came suddenly—and quite unexpectedly—but not so abruptly as to leave him without the opportunity to record his final words. As mentioned in chapter 3, Machen finished grading his papers and wrapped up the details at Westminster Theological Seminary for the close of the term and then boarded a train to North Dakota. The reason? One of the congregations in the fledgling denomination, started just six months prior, faced difficulty and challenge. Machen, worn down from exhaustion of body and soul, disregarded the pleas of his seminary colleagues and headed west.

He preached, listened, and counseled, and in the process, facing the cruel North Dakota winter, he contracted pneumonia, from which he was not to recover. A doctor had him hospitalized. Two days later, on New Year's Day 1937, he died. His last three days were difficult ones of intense suffering, and his last day passed with extended moments of unconsciousness. In a time of lucidity, however, Machen, sensing that the end was near, sent a telegram to his trusted colleague and professor of systematic theology at Westminster Theological Seminary, John Murray. It read, "I am so thankful for [the] active obedience of Christ. No hope without it." Machen's impending death gave him a clarity to lay out the breadth and the depth of the gospel that he had lived his life embracing and defending.

There is a context that further explains these last words, and even explains why he sent the telegram to John Murray. In addition to concluding the work of the fall term before he left for North Dakota, Machen also finished up his radio broadcasts for the year just before he left. For the past few years, Machen's voice could be regularly heard on radio station WIP in Philadelphia, an attempt both to give exposure to the seminary and to provide solid teaching in a time when the gospel was threatened. Machen's radio talks constitute a primer on basic theology. He began with the doctrine of the Bible, moving on to the doctrine of God. Machen gathered those talks together, publishing them with

Macmillan in 1936 under the title *The Christian Faith in the Modern World*. He followed up those talks with a series on the doctrine of humanity, with "a considerable part of the discussion . . . concerned with what the Bible says about sin." Machen prepared these talks for publication as well, and they were in the hands of Macmillan when he died, published in the spring of 1937 under the title *The Christian View of Man*. He had just started in the fall of 1936 a series on the doctrine of salvation, beginning with the work of Christ on the cross.

Those listening to WIP during the four Sundays in December 1936 heard Machen patiently walking them through the glories of the work of Christ as our priest, through his death on the cross gaining our access to God. He prerecorded the last one, which aired on December 27, 1936, before he boarded the train to North Dakota. This chapter explores the depths of those four messages delivered in December. They not only explain the telegram's cryptic reference, but also go a long way toward giving us a clear view of the purpose and meaning of the life of J. Gresham Machen. Perhaps more than any other text, these messages reveal who Machen was and what he was about.

Conversations over the Air

Machen's response in 1908 to the fact that he would someday in the future be regularly broadcasting sermons over the radio would have been at first laughter and then concerted disbelief. That year finds Machen, as a professor at Princeton, nervously sweating about giving a chapel sermon. He had been supposed to give one in prior years, as expected of all faculty members, but because of the surplus of faculty and students wanting to preach and because of Machen's not asserting his privilege to preach, he had been passed over. It caught up with him in 1908. On the morning he was scheduled to preach, Machen anxiously sat in his room, perched on the third floor of Alexander Hall. He could look out his window, across the manicured lawns and hearty elms and oaks of the seminary grounds, and see the students filing in past the imposing columns guarding the entrance to Miller Chapel. Meanwhile, Machen was doing anything to distract himself. He resorted to his favorite pastime; the final moments found him "writing letters vigorously to keep my courage up." That was in 1908. By 1936, and many sermons later, Machen was quite at home in the pulpit, as well as at the classroom lectern. And those who heard his sermons found something worth listening to.

Letters expressing gratitude for his sermons preached at Miller Chapel and many pulpits elsewhere fill his files of correspondence. One letter, from A. Russell Stevenson, came to Machen after he had given a sermon in the chapel at Union College in Schenectady, New York, in 1920. The letter also reveals a bit of Machen's style in the pulpit, as Stevenson writes, having missed the opportunity to personally relay these remarks to Machen at the door: "I wanted to thank you for the great address you gave us—great in the simplicity of its method and play of humor, and great in its analysis of the duty of the church in ministering to the soul by telling it the great fact of Jesus." He then offered the true test of effectiveness by relating, "My son came home so enthusiastic that he talked for half an hour about the point you made and the masterly way in which you did it." He closed by encouraging Machen to "talk on that theme whenever you have a chance." Quite fitting it is that at the time of his death Machen was talking on the theme of Christ and his work. The letter further reveals that Machen possessed the rare quality of speaking in a compelling way to both scholars and laity alike.

EIGHTH ANNUAL OPENING EXERCISES

of

WESTMINSTER THEOLOGICAL SEMINARY

WEDNESDAY, SEPTEMBER 30, 1936

at three o'clock

WITHERSPOON AUDITORIUM

REV. PROFESSOR J. GRESHAM MACHEN, D.D., Litt.D.
Chairman of the Faculty, Presiding

DOXOLOGY

INVOCATION
Rev. John B. Thwing, Th.D.

HYMN

Christ is made the sure Foundation,
Christ the Head and Cornerstone,
Chosen of the Lord and precious,
Binding all the Church in one;
Holy Zion's help for ever,
And her confidence alone.

All that dedicated city,
Dearly loved of God on high,
In exultant jubilation
Pours perpetual melody;
God the One in Three adoring
In glad hymns eternally.

Here vouchsafe to all Thy servants
What they ask of Thee to gain,
What they gain from Thee for ever
With the blessed to retain,
And hereafter in Thy glory
Evermore with Thee to reign.

Laud and honor to the Father,
Laud and honor to the Son,
Laud and honor to the Spirit,
Ever Three and ever One,
One in might, and One in glory,
While unending ages run.

READING OF THE SCRIPTURE
Rev. Franklin S. Dyrness

PRAYER
Rev. Carl McIntire

ANNOUNCEMENTS

GREETING TO THE ENTERING STUDENTS
Dr. Machen

HYMN

God is my strong Salvation;
What foe have I to fear?
In darkness and temptation
My Light, my Help is near.

Though hosts encamp around me,
Firm to the fight I stand,
What terror can confound me,
With God at my right hand?

Place on the Lord reliance,
My soul, with courage wait;
His truth be thine affiance,
When faint and desolate.

His might thy heart shall strengthen,
His love thy joy increase;
Mercy thy days shall lengthen;
The Lord will give thee peace.

ADDRESS—"Thank God and Take Courage"
Rev. H. Henry Meeter, Th.D.
Professor of Bible in Calvin College

PRAYER
Rev. Alexander K. Davison

HYMN

Supreme in wisdom as in power
The Rock of Ages stands;
Though Him thou canst not see, nor trace
The working of His hands.

He gives the conquest to the weak,
Supports the fainting heart;
And courage in the evil hour
His heavenly aids impart.

Mere human power shall fast decay,
And youthful vigor cease;
But they who wait upon the Lord
In strength shall still increase.

On eagles' wings they mount, they soar,
Their wings are faith and love,
Till, past the cloudy regions here,
They rise to heaven above.

BENEDICTION

12.1. Program for the opening exercises of Westminster Seminary in 1936. Machen would not live through the completion of the school year.

His ability to cast a sermon "in the simplicity of its method" largely accounts for why he made a good candidate to speak over the radio in 1935 and 1936. In fact, Machen came to enjoy his conversations over the air, as he relays in his last talk on the doctrine of God, later published in *The Christian Faith in the Modern World:* "In bringing this little series to a close, I want to say what a great pleasure it has been to me to become acquainted with you. Our conversations might, indeed, seem at first sight to have been just a little bit one-sided; in them I have done most of the talking." He added a touch of dry humor: "I hope you will not be unkind enough to say that that is the reason why I have enjoyed the conversations so much." The real reason he enjoyed the conversations lay elsewhere, in "the companionship that I have had with you." He explains, "These are rather trying days to a man who sorrows when a visible church that professes to believe the Word of God turns from it so often into the pathways of unbelief and sin; and in such days it is doubly comforting to converse with those who truly love the Gospel of Christ and believe that it alone is the message forever new." More than fellowship with like-minded believers was the goal of the radio talks. Machen frequently ends his talks with pleas for those outside of Christ to come to him. Painted as a bully or as an instigator of trouble by his detractors and enemies, Machen reveals in these talks the warmth and affability that so many attested to and that so characterized his life.

The way in which Machen constructed these talks also informs us of a great deal of his life's work. He structured the series around the Westminster Shorter Catechism. Though the catechism serves as the backbone for the series, rarely if ever does Machen explicitly refer to it. Instead, he uses it as a guide to lay a solid foundation and superstructure of sound biblical teaching. Machen starts with the Bible, arguing for its authority and truthfulness, as the only sure and reliable guide to understanding God and the world and our place in it. He then moves on to the doctrine of God, not shrinking away from the doctrines of the Trinity and the deity of Christ as so many others in his day were doing. Next, he challenges the naive view of human nature permeating modern sensibilities in his series on the doctrine of humanity and sin. He captures the twin teachings of the dignity of humanity, stemming from the image of God within and not from some trumped-up sense of the self, and the depravity of humanity, flowing from the imputation of Adam's sin and everywhere revealed in the deceitfulness of our own hearts and our plaguing selfishness. Weeks and months of patient instruction set the stage for the very talks that came in December 1936 and the ones that he planned to give in 1937 exhibiting the glorious work of Christ on our behalf and God's gracious gift of salvation. In short, these talks, aimed at the casual hearer, are doctrinal to the core.

In one of his talks from the fall of 1936, entitled "The Creeds and Doctrinal Advance," Machen addresses the tendency of the day to disregard doctrine, relying on sentiment and experience instead, familiar themes to readers of Machen. In the process, he refers to the maxim of Archimedes, "Give me a place to stand, and I will move the world." To Machen, the fulcrum was doctrine, as he notes, "Christian doctrine provides that place to stand." From that stance comes true progress; all else "is an illusion." Machen then set off to explore—although, of course, he had no idea at the time—what was to be his last doctrinal discussion, the work of Christ on the cross.

Christ Our High Priest

"That Christ died, and that he died for me," were words often found in the writings of J. Gresham Machen, and words he loved to proclaim from the pulpit. They also epitomize the last four radio talks he gave, "Christ Our Redeemer," "The Doctrine of the Atonement," "The Active Obedience of Christ," and "The Bible and the Cross," all published in *God Transcendent*. These talks constitute the mere beginnings of his treatment of the doctrine of salvation, which he commences by looking at the work of Christ. To do so, he enlists the aid of the helpful construct of Christ's three offices or functions as prophet, priest, and king. These three offices capture the vast biblical teaching on Christ's work, and the four talks at hand deal with his role as our high priest. In summary, Machen makes the point that "Christ made the one all-sufficient sacrifice for sin," adding, "Nothing, from the point of view of the Bible, can possibly be more important for mankind than that."

Christ's work as priest, however, assumes that we are in need of a priest. This leads Machen to explain that priests serve to grant access to God. Humanity's sin, and inability to overcome it, creates an absolute dependence upon a priest who can accomplish that task and grant the necessary access to God for sinners separated from him. It is no assumption, in other words, that humanity is in need of such a priest; it is a dire need. Through Christ's priestly work on the cross, we gain access to God and are reconciled to him. This summary comes in the first talk, "Christ Our Redeemer." Machen spends the next three talks further explaining and expanding these points.

The work of Christ on the cross, as Machen tells his audience, is commonly referred to as the doctrine of the atonement. The word *atonement*, though occurring only once in the New Testament, occurs throughout the Old Testament to refer to "the sacrifice that God is pleased to accept in order that man may again be received into favour." Machen puts the implication of the doctrine of the atonement even more directly when he speaks of "the death of Christ as something that was necessary in order that sinful man might be received into communion with God." Machen also uses the term *satisfaction* to communicate the effects of this work of Christ because his death on the cross, and life of perfect obedience, fully satisfied the wrath of God and earned our entrance into heaven.

Sin, both the original sin of Adam for which we are under penalty at birth and our own individual sin, cuts us off from God, leaving us further without the ability to earn forgiveness. But Christ is our substitute, and when he "died upon the cross, he made full satisfaction for our sins; he paid the penalty which the law pronounces upon our sin, not in part but in full." And of course, given the deity of Christ, "God himself," as Machen observes, "paid the penalty of sin—God Himself in the Person of God the Son, who loved us and gave Himself for us." In fact, he further explains the Trinitarian work of God in salvation, noting that not only Christ's work accomplished salvation but also the work of "God Himself in the Person of God the Father who so loved the world as to give His only-begotten Son, God the Holy Spirit who applies to us the benefits of Christ's death. God's the cost and ours the marvelous gain!"

This, Machen acknowledges, constitutes one particular view of the atonement, the substutionary view. This view, the orthodox view of the church, faced challenges in Machen's day. Alongside of that view, as Machen explains, the moral-influence and the governmental theories of the atonement were also placed. In the moral-influence theory, "Christ's death upon the cross had merely a moral effect upon man." Through it, we too can be selfless and sacrificial and loving—all the things that God honored in Christ and that he will honor in us when we follow his example. The governmental theory puts a slight twist on this in its view of the demand to punish sin as providing "an adequate deterrent from sinning." Not only were these theories rampant in Machen's day, especially the moral-influence theory, there were many who held that debating the theories proved no worthwhile task. "People sometimes say," Machen observes, "that it makes little difference what theory of the atonement we hold." Machen just as quickly points out, however, that "it makes all the difference in the world." Further, he proclaims that only one theory adequately reflects the Bible's teaching—the substitutionary view of the atonement. The repercussions of rejecting it are enormous.

The moral-influence theory of Christ's death reflects a fundamentally different perspective on the person of Christ from that of the substitutionary theory. Consequently, the moral-influence view reflects something altogether different from orthodox, biblical Christianity. Machen expresses it this way in *Christianity and Liberalism:* "What then is the difference between liberalism and Christianity with regard to the person of our Lord? . . . [L]iberalism regards Jesus as the fairest flower of humanity; Christianity regards him as a supernatural person." Perhaps no better illustration can be found of this view of the person of Christ "as the fairest flower of humanity" and the way it infects the view of Christ's work than that of Henry van Dyke and his best-selling Christmas tale from 1896 and still popular in the 1930s, *The Other Wise Man,* the book that was instrumental in winning van Dyke a place on the literature faculty at Princeton University. Van Dyke, it may be recalled, was also at the center of the controversy at First Presbyterian Church

1933

REV. PROFESSOR J. GRESHAM MACHEN, D.D., Litt.D.

of

WESTMINSTER THEOLOGICAL SEMINARY

will speak on

"CONSISTENT CHRISTIANITY"

over

STATION WIP — 610 KILOCYCLES

in the

Central-North Broad Street Presbyterian Church
Broad and Green Streets
Philadelphia

Sunday, March 5th
8 P. M. to 9 P. M.

12.2. An advertisement for an address by Machen on radio station WIP. The same station broadcast Machen's final sermons on the four Sundays in December, 1936.

in Princeton, publicly relinquishing his pew because of Machen's preaching.

The Other Wise Man recounts the fictional exploits of Artaban, always one step behind in his quest to meet Jesus. During his long and circuitous journey, the various gifts he carries to lay before Jesus dwindle, except for a lone "soft and iridescent" pearl. Artaban makes one last trip to Jerusalem, thirty-three years after he began his quest. It happens to be Passover. In yet another strange turn of events, he ends up ransoming a young girl with his pearl, struggling over "the expectation of faith and the impulse of love," and resolving the conflict in rhetorically asking, "And is not love the light of the soul?" At the very moment, we are to assume, Christ is dying on the cross, and Artaban finds salvation "because he had done the best that he could from day to day. He had been true to the light that had been given to him." Christ's death recedes into the background. In fact, it was not Christ's death that saved Artaban. Rather, Christ's selfless act merely inspired Artaban to do the same. When Machen challenges his readers to read "most of the popular books on religion of the present day," which teach merely "that Christ on Calvary pointed out a way that we follow . . . hallow[ing] the pathway of self-sacrifice," he had books such as van Dyke's in mind.

The problem with van Dyke and other adherents of the moral-influence theory, according to Machen, is that "they are wrong in not observing clearly that fallen man, dead in trespasses and sins, can never be made to live a holy life merely by the introduction of new motives or new incentives to goodness." The moral-influence theory both robs Christ's work of its value and wrongly places that value on the side of human ability and accomplishment. Machen puts the tragic consequences this way: "He loves little to whom little is forgiven," continuing, "If the sin for which we are forgiven is merely the light, easily forgiven thing that the advocates of the moral-influence theory of the atonement think it is, then no great spring of gratitude will well up in our souls toward Him who has caused us to be forgiven." But "if it is the profound and deadly thing that the advocates of the substitutionary view of the atonement think it is, then all our lives will be one song of gratitude to Him who loved us and gave Himself for us on the accursed tree." This latter view overflows the pages of the Bible. One further dimension to Christ's priestly work concerns his obedience, both passive and active. Machen takes up this topic in his next-to-last sermon, delivered on December 20, 1936.

The Active Obedience of Christ

The third talk, "The Active Obedience of Christ," explains the telegram containing Machen's last words. For this talk, he sought counsel and input from his colleague John Murray, who had been educated at Princeton and taught there for a year before joining Machen on the Westminster faculty in 1930. In the early years of the seminary the two forged quite a bond, enjoying a number of hearty theological discussions. One such discussion came just before Machen's death as he was preparing his talk on the active obedience of Christ. With vivid memories of that final discussion in view, Machen directed his last telegram to the young professor of theology. That explains the recipient of the telegram; it remains to explain the content of the message.

Machen contrasts the active with the passive obedience of Christ. Christ's passive obedience pays the penalty of our sin. While that alone is cause to rejoice, it still leaves a dilemma. With only the penalty of sin paid, we are essentially back where Adam started, still in a state of probation, needing to merit perfect obedience to the law of God. The guilt is removed, but then we are left "to our own efforts to win the reward which God has pronounced upon perfect obedience," the reward of eternal life. But, Machen declares, "I must really decline to speculate any further," adding, "As a matter of fact, [Christ] has not merely paid the penalty of Adam's first sin, and the penalty of the sins which we have individually committed, but He also has positively merited for us eternal life." We need to see Christ's work of both passive and active obedience. The passive obedience of Christ pays the penalty; the active obedience merits the reward of eternal life. Christ accomplished this work on our behalf on the cross, and there is, as Machen relays in the telegram, "no hope without it."

The terminology of the active and passive obedience of Christ helps us see, according to Machen, that Christ suffered in our stead, saving us from the penalty of death, and that he also was actively obedient "to what the law of God required" in his perfect righteousness, meriting for us the reward of life. This is the great accomplishment to which this terminology refers. "Yet," Machen adds, "a danger lurks in it if it leads us to think that one of the two parts of Christ's work can be separated from the other." Neither is it helpful to see the active obedience as related to his life and the passive obedience related to his death on the cross. As Machen notes, "every event of His life was both active obedience and passive obedience." Machen then offers this summary:

> We can put it briefly by saying that Christ took our place with respect to the law of God. He paid for us the law's penalty, and He obeyed for us the law's commands. He saved us from hell, and He earned for us our entrance into heaven. All that we have, then, we owe unto Him. There is no blessing that we have in this world or the next for which we should not give Christ thanks.

Now we understand why he sent those last words to Murray. And we understand why he was so thankful for the active obedience of Christ.

Conclusion

Machen closed his broadcast on December 27, 1936, with these words: "On this last Sunday of the old year, I just want to say to you who have been listening in on these Sunday afternoons how much encouraged I have been by your Christian fellowship." He went on to say, "I trust that you have had a very joyous Christmas and I trust that the new year which is so soon to begin may be to you a very blessed year under the mercy of God." It is intriguing to speculate what the next broadcast would have brought. Machen promised his audience that he would walk them through specific biblical passages on the death of Christ, beginning with "that great passage in the tenth chapter of the Gospel according to Mark, where our Lord says that the Son of Man came to give His life a ransom for many." It doubtless would have been worth hearing. But the opportunity did not come, and Machen's work in the new year did not proceed past its first day.

Nevertheless, we have quite a body of material that Machen did manage to leave behind for generations to come. While some of that material is directly aimed at New Testament scholars or at theologians, all of it was intended for the church. His work had a profound impact on the generation in which it was first delivered, and it can potentially do the same for this and even future generations. In this chapter, as we did in the last one, we merely skimmed the surface of a significant portion of that work in the legacy of his sermons. These few sermons considered, however, demonstrate why his work had such impact—Machen pointed his generation, and by extension ours as well, to the cross of Christ.

A Note on the Sources

The four sermons "Christ Our Redeemer," "The Doctrine of the Atonement," "The Active Obedience of Christ," and "The Bible and the Cross" may be found in J. Gresham Machen, *God Transcendent,* edited by Ned B. Stonehouse (1982), 168–206. Henry van Dyke's *The Story of the Other Wise Man,* first published by Harper in 1895, has been reprinted numerous times. For a brief discussion of Machen's preaching, see Henry W. Coray, *J. Gresham Machen* (1981), 60–64. For Machen's last days and his trip to North Dakota, see Ned B. Stonehouse, *J. Gresham Machen* (1987), 493–508. For additional sermons and radio addresses of Machen, see his *The Christian Faith in the Modern World* (1936, reprinted 1965) and *The Christian View of Man* (1937, reprinted 1965).

CONTINUING THE JOURNEY: A SELECT GUIDE TO BOOKS BY AND ABOUT J. GRESHAM MACHEN

As mentioned in the introduction, this book is intended merely as a gateway into the writings of J. Gresham Machen. Most of his major books and a number of his significant essays have been discussed in the earlier chapters in order to provide a context for those writings. This has not been an exhaustive treatment, and it by no means professes to be the final word on Machen. But if it serves to prompt further reading and exploration, then it has fulfilled its purpose. In these last few pages, some further guidance is offered in order to help those who want to keep on exploring more of the fruitful life and work of J. Gresham Machen. For those who do, the journey is well worthwhile.

Books by Machen

Most of the major books by Machen are in print. And those not currently in print can still be found fairly readily. Perhaps the book to begin with is Machen's classic work, *Christianity and Liberalism*. Machen's astute thought and clear writing, as well as the perennial nature of the issues involved in the book's subject matter, all contribute to making the book a classic among theological literature and a valuable text for understanding twentieth-century and contemporary religious history, especially in America. His book *What Is Faith?*, essentially a sequel to *Christianity and Liberalism*, might be the next place to turn.

Students of Machen should remember, however, that these books (from 1923 and 1925, respectively) do not engage Machen's thought coming out of the controversy at Princeton Seminary or his ouster from the Presbyterian Church in the U.S.A. For the best treatment of that period, as well as the most comprehensive treatment of the entire breadth and scope of Machen's work, see J. Gresham Machen's *Selected Shorter Writings*, edited by D. G. Hart (2004). This book, which contains at its center *What Is Christianity? And Other Addresses* (1951), edited by Ned B. Stonehouse and first published in 1951, brings together a number of significant essays and addresses, book reviews, and articles. Hart's introduction also serves well to grasp the full picture of Machen's thought. The two books of sermons, *The Christian View of Man* and *God Transcendent*, edited by Ned B. Stonehouse, are also rewarding.

Machen's works in New Testament scholarship, *The Origin of Paul's Religion* and *The Virgin Birth of Christ*, though outdated by today's standards of scholarship, still prove worthwhile, the latter book remaining the most thorough and scholarly conservative treatment of the New Testament birth narratives of Christ. The views of Wilhelm Bousset, on which Machen spends a great deal of time in *The Origin of Paul's Religion*, still garner interest. Consequently, Machen's critique well repays reading. Another of Machen's contributions to New Testament studies was *Machen's Notes on Galatians* (1977), edited by John H. Skilton, one of Machen's students. Machen's *New Testament Greek for Be-*

ginners is still available for those wanting to learn New Testament Greek. Machen's various lessons prepared for the Presbyterian Board of Christian Education have been gathered together in J. Gresham Machen, *The New Testament: An Introduction to Its Literature and History* (1976), edited by W. John Cook.

A full bibliography of Machen's writings, including the various reprints of his books and articles up to 1984, was prepared by James T. Dennison and Grace Mullen and may be found in *Pressing Toward the Mark: Essays Commemorating Fifty Years of the Orthodox Presbyterian Church* (1986).

Books about Machen

The classic biography remains Ned B. Stonehouse's *J. Gresham Machen: A Biographical Memoir* (1954, 2004). Stonehouse, Machen's younger colleague in New Testament, spent many years combing through the archives, publishing essays and addresses of Machen, and preparing his biography. A good complement to Stonehouse is D. G. Hart's intellectual biography, *Defending the Faith: J. Gresham Machen and the Crisis of Conservative Protestantism in America* (1994). His book, as well as his many essays, is indispensable to understanding Machen. More recently, Terry A. Chrisope has offered a thorough treatment of the formative earlier years of Machen in his *Toward a Sure Faith: J. Gresham Machen and the Dilemma of Biblical Criticism, 1881–1915* (2000).

Two other shorter works, both by authors who had direct contact with Machen, also provide helpful portraits of his life. Henry W. Coray's *J. Gresham Machen: A Silhouette* (1981) offers vignettes of the various roles Machen played and of the episodes of his life. Paul Woolley's *The Signifi-*

cance of J. Gresham Machen Today (1977) depicts "the living man at his work."

To understand Machen, it is helpful to understand Princeton Theological Seminary. For that, David Calhoun's two-volume *Princeton Seminary* (1994, 1996) is indispensable. It is also helpful to understand the modernist controversy. Perhaps these three books help the best, with their particular focus on Machen: Bradley J. Longfield, *The Presbyterian Controversy: Fundamentalists, Modernists, and Moderates* (1991); George M. Marsden, *Understanding Fundamentalism and Evangelicalism* (1991); and Edwin H. Rian, *The Presbyterian Conflict* (1992). For an insightful treatment of the Orthodox Presbyterian Church, including some direct discussions of Machen, see *Pressing Toward the Mark,* edited by Charles G. Dennison and Richard C. Gamble (1986). A helpful guide to keeping all the names straight is the *Dictionary of the Presbyterian and Reformed Tradition in America,* edited by D. G. Hart and Mark A. Noll (1999).

BIBLIOGRAPHY

Berkhof, Hendrikus. *Two Hundred Years of Theology: Report of a Personal Journey.* Translated by John Vriend. Grand Rapids: Eerdmans, 1989.

Calhoun, David B. *Princeton Seminary.* 2 vols. Edinburgh/Carlisle, Pa.: Banner of Truth, 1994–1996.

Chrisope, Terry A. *Toward a Sure Faith: J. Gresham Machen and the Dilemma of Biblical Criticism, 1881–1915.* Fearn (Ross-shire): Mentor, 2000.

Churchill, Robert King. *Lest We Forget: A Personal Reflection of the Formation of the Orthodox Presbyterian Church.* Philadelphia: Committee for the Historian of the Orthodox Presbyterian Church, 1986.

Coray, Henry W. *J. Gresham Machen: A Silhouette.* Grand Rapids: Kregel, 1981.

Dennison, Charles G. *History for a Pilgrim People: The Historical Writings of Charles G. Dennison.* Edited by Danny E. Olinger and David K. Thompson. Willow Grove, Pa.: Committee for the Historian of the Orthodox Presbyterian Church, 2002.

———, and Richard C. Gamble, eds. *Pressing Toward the Mark: Essays Commemorating Fifty Years of the Orthodox Presbyterian Church.* Philadelphia: Committee for the Historian of the Orthodox Presbyterian Church, 1986.

Dennison, James T., and Grace Mullen. "A Bibliography of the Writings of J. Gresham Machen, 1881–1937." In *Pressing Toward the Mark: Essays Commemorating Fifty Years of the Orthodox Presbyterian Church,* 461–85. Philadelphia: Committee for the Historian of the Orthodox Presbyterian Church, 1986.

Dorrien, Gary. *The Making of American Liberal Theology: Idealism, Realism, and Modernity, 1900–1950.* Louisville, Ky.: Westminster John Knox, 2003.

———. *The Making of American Liberal Theology: Imagining Progressive Religion, 1805–1900.* Louisville, Ky.: Westminster John Knox, 2001.

DuBois, W. E. B. *The Souls of Black Folk*. Chicago: A. C. McClurg, 1903. Reprint ed. Boston: Bedford Books, 1997.

Fosdick, Harry Emerson. *The Challenge of the Present Crisis*. New York: Association, 1917.

———. "Shall the Fundamentalists Win?" In *American Sermons: The Pilgrims to Martin Luther King, Jr.*, edited by Michael Warner, 775–86. New York: Library of America, 1999.

Harries, Meirion and Susie. *The Last Days of Innocence: America at War, 1917–1918*. New York: Random House, 1997.

Harrisville, Roy A., and Walter Sundberg. *The Bible in Modern Culture: Theology and Historical-Critical Method from Spinoza to Käsemann*. Grand Rapids: Eerdmans, 1995.

Hart, D. G. *Defending the Faith: J. Gresham Machen and the Crisis of Conservative Protestantism in Modern America*. Baltimore: Johns Hopkins University, 1994.

Hart, D. G., and Mark A. Noll, eds. *Dictionary of the Presbyterian and Reformed Tradition in America*. Downers Grove, Ill.: InterVarsity, 1999.

Howard, Michael. *The First World War*. Oxford/New York: Oxford University, 2002.

Hutchison, William R. *The Modernist Impulse in American Protestantism*. Cambridge, Mass.: Harvard University, 1976. Reprint ed. Durham, N. C.: Duke University, 1992.

Longfield, Bradley J. *The Presbyterian Controversy: Fundamentalists, Modernists, and Moderates*. New York: Oxford University, 1991.

Macartney, Clarence Edward. "Shall Unbelief Win? An Answer to Dr. Fosdick." In *Sermons That Shaped America: Reformed Preaching from 1630 to 2001*, edited by William S. Barker and Samuel T. Logan Jr., 323–43. Phillipsburg, N. J.: P&R, 2003.

Machen, Arthur W. *Letters of Arthur W. Machen with Biographical Sketch*. Compiled by Arthur W. Machen Jr. Baltimore: n.p., 1917.

Machen, J. Gresham. *The Christian Faith in the Modern World*. New York: Macmillan, 1936. Reprint ed. Grand Rapids: Eerdmans, 1965.

———. *The Christian View of Man*. New York: Macmillan, 1937. Reprint ed. London: Banner of Truth, 1965.

———. *Christianity and Liberalism*. New York: Macmillan, 1923. Reprint ed. Grand Rapids: Eerdmans, 1946.

———. *Education, Christianity and the State*. 2d ed. Edited by John W. Robbins. Hobbs, N. M.: Trinity Foundation, 1995.

———. *God Transcendent*. Edited by Ned B. Stonehouse. Grand Rapids: Eerdmans, 1949. Reprint ed. Edinburgh/Carlisle, Pa.: Banner of Truth, 1982.

————. *Machen's Notes on Galatians: Notes on Biblical Exposition and Other Aids to the Interpretation of the Epistle to the Galatians.* 2d ed. Edited by John H. Skilton. Nutley, N. J.: P&R, 1977.

————. Modernism and the Board of Foreign Missions of the Presbyterian Church in the U.S.A. Philadelphia: n.p., 1933.

————. *New Testament Greek for Beginners.* New York: Macmillan, 1923. 2d ed. Revised by Dan G. McCartney. Upper Saddle Rivers, N. J.: Pearson Prentice Hall, 2004.

————. *The New Testament: An Introduction to Its Literature and History.* Edited by W. John Cook. Edinburgh/Carlisle, Pa.: Banner of Truth, 1976.

————. *The Origin of Paul's Religion.* New York: Macmillan, 1921. Reprint ed. Eugene, Ore.: Wipf and Stock, 2002.

————. "The God of the Early Christians." Review. *Princeton Theological Review,* 22 (1924): 544–88.

————. *Selected Shorter Writings.* Edited by D. G. Hart. Phillipsburg, N. J.: P&R, 2004.

————. *Statement to the Special Committee of the Presbytery of New Brunswick.* Philadelphia: J. Gresham Machen, 1934.

————. *The Virgin Birth of Christ.* New York: Harper, 1930. Reprint eds. Grand Rapids: Baker, 1965 and Cambridge: J. Clarke, 2000.

————. *What Is Christianity? And Other Addresses.* Edited by Ned B. Stonehouse. Grand Rapids: Eerdmans, 1951.

————. *What Is Faith?* New York: Macmillan, 1925. Reprint ed. Edinburgh/Carlisle, Pa.: Banner of Truth Trust, 1991.

Marsden, George M. *Fundamentalism and American Culture: The Shaping of Twentieth Century Evangelicalism, 1870–1925.* New York: Oxford University, 1980.

————. *The Soul of the American University: From Protestant Establishment to Established Nonbelief.* New York: Oxford University, 1994.

————. *Understanding Fundamentalism and Evangelicalism.* Grand Rapids: Eerdmans, 1991.

Michael, C. Richard, "The Fundamentalist-Modernist Controversy and the Work of J. Gresham Machen: Lessons for Evangelicalism Today," M.A.B. Thesis, Lancaster Bible College Graduate School, 2003.

Noll, Mark A. *Between Faith and Criticism: Evangelicals, Scholarship, and the Bible in America.* San Francisco: Harper & Row, 1986.

Rian, Edwin H. *The Presbyterian Conflict.* Grand Rapids: Eerdmans, 1940. Reprint ed. Philadelphia: Committee for the Historian of the Orthodox Presbyterian Church, 1992.

Stonehouse, Ned B. *J. Gresham Machen: A Biographical Memoir.* Grand Rapids: Eerdmans, 1954. Reprint ed. Willow Grove, Pa.: Committee for the Historian of the Orthodox Presbyterian Church, 2004.

Van Dyke, Henry. *The Story of the Other Wise Man.* New York: Harper, 1895. Reprint ed. New York: Ballantine, 1996.

Woolley, Paul. *The Significance of J. Gresham Machen Today.* Nutley, N. J.: P&R, 1977.

Zieger, Robert H. *America's Great War: World War I and the American Experience.* Lanham, Md.: Rowman & Littlefield, 2000.

INDEX OF PERSONS

Index of Machen's Works

Stephen J. Nichols (M.A.R. and Ph.D., Westminster Theological Seminary; M.A., West Chester University) is an associate professor at Lancaster Bible College and Graduate School. A member of the Evangelical Theological Society, he chairs the society's Jonathan Edwards Study Group. He is also author of *Jonathan Edwards: A Guided Tour of His Life and Thought, Martin Luther: A Guided Tour of His Life and Thought, An Absolute Sort of Certainty: The Holy Spirit and the Apologetics of Jonathan Edwards,* and coeditor of *The Legacy of Jonathan Edwards: American Religion and the Evangelical Tradition.*